# HAVING
# FUN
# WITH
# AGILITY

## Also by Margaret H. Bonham from Howell Book House

*The Complete Guide to Mutts: Selection, Care, and Celebration from Puppyhood to Senior*

# HAVING
# FUN
# WITH
# AGILITY

MARGARET H. BONHAM

HOWELL
BOOK
HOUSE

*Library of Congress Cataloging-in-Publication Data:*

Bonham, Margaret H.
  Having fun with agility / by Margaret Bonham.
     p. cm.
  Includes bibliographical references.
  ISBN 0-7645-7298-9 (alk. paper)
  1. Dogs—Agility trials. 2. Dogs—Training. I. Title.
  SF425.4.B658 2004
  636.7'0835—dc22
                                        2004014425
Printed in the United States of America

10  9  8  7  6  5  4  3  2  1

Book design by LeAndra Hosier
Cover design by Wendy Mount
Book production by Wiley Publishing, Inc. Composition Services

*In loving memory of Snopeak Kiana of Sky Warrior
NA U-AGI, WTD, WPD, CGC my agility dog, best friend,
and booksigner. And to Belle's Lachlan's Black Dragon, aka,
Haegl, an up-and-coming agility Malamute and all-around
troublemaker, and to Larry, who gives constant support.*

# Contents

Acknowledgments                                              ix

Introduction                                                 1

Part One: Learning Agility

1   Getting Started                                          5

2   Clicker for Fun (Learning the Rules)                    23

3   Clicking with Agility (Obstacle Training)               45

4   Handling Your Dog                                       67

Part Two: Having Fun and Playing Games

5   Fun Games and Courses                                   83

6   Holding an Agility Party                               101

Part Three: Health and Agility

7   Emphasizing Good Health                                119

8   Nutrition for Your Agility Dog                         131

9   Having Fun with Special-Needs Dogs                     141

Part Four: What's Ahead—Getting Involved

10 Where to Go from Here 151

Appendix A: Agility Organizations 165

Appendix B: Agility References 171

Picture Credits 175

Index 177

# Acknowledgments

I would like to thank the following people for their help with this book: Jessica Faust of Bookends; Kathy Nebenhaus, publisher, John Wiley & Sons; Cindy Kitchel, director of aquisitions; Chris Stambaugh, editorial manager; Roxane Cerda, aquisitions editor; Dale Cunningham, acquisitions editor; Sharon Sakson, developmental editor; Lisa Burstiner, production editor; Larry Bonham, who helped keep me sane and helped with the photos; and Beth Adelman for advice throughout.

I would also like to thank the following people and dogs who appeared in this book (or who supplied photos): Margaret Meleski and JD; Stephanie Podejkov and TJ; Jim and Kathy Stabler and Robyn; Joyce Tessler and Gideon; Jeanne Grim and Demi; Pam Metzger and Sableman; Lisa Dewey and Vapor and Rush; Sue Johnson and Zippy; Teresa Bullard and Ginger, Cinnamon, and Audrey; Becky Thompson and Molly; Lisa Kretner; Ed Kelley; Kenneth Reed; Pet Action Shots; Nancy Latthitham; Tien Tran Photography; Steve Surfman; Sharon Sakson; Roger Greenwald; BinnsPhotography.com; Ceyn Van Leeuwen; and Amy Kluth.

Lastly, I want to thank my dogs whom I learned so much from.

# Introduction

Agility is the fastest-growing dog sport in the country. You've probably heard about agility on TV or through training classes from your local obedience trainer. Maybe you saw an agility competition at a dog show. Those dogs look cool blazing through weave poles, over A-frames, and across dog walks.

Not my dog, you think. But why not?

There may be lots of reasons why you think your dog can't do this. Maybe he's a couch potato. Perhaps he's a mixed breed from the pound. Maybe he's never learned to sit or come when you call. Or you think he's too big, too small, too old, or too young. But maybe it's the competition.

Agility originally appeared at the famous Cruft's Dog Show in Britain in 1978 as entertainment. Not a sport. Entertainment. The dogs were there to wow the audiences, and they did. Naturally, everyone wanted to try agility, and soon people were training their dogs to do extraordinary things like run across A-frames and through tunnels. Somewhere along the line, agility turned from fun to competition. Competition became intense, and more people started concentrating on times and developing their dog's abilities, and they forgot that—not *if*—they were having fun. Consequently, much of the talk about agility is about trials and training and clean runs. People now choose dogs based on their breed and agility aptitude rather than being a cool pet.

When I got into agility with Kiana, my white Malamute, organized agility was just starting in Colorado. There were few rules and regulations then, although we had an inkling of what the future would hold. People showed up with mixed breeds and unusual breeds like Malamutes, Huskies, Great Danes, Dalmatians, Boxers, Bulldogs, and even Bassett Hounds. Training was mostly on-leash and everyone was there to have fun.

The neat thing about agility is that you still can have fun. You don't need to know the latest AKC rules to learn obstacle training. You don't have to yell at your dog when he isn't sitting properly on the table or worry if he touches the contacts. So, you don't have to have your dog off leash. Call-offs, refusals, and off courses don't matter, and you're not looking for blistering times. Instead, you're having fun.

What fun can you have with agility if you throw out the rulebooks? Plenty! Your dog doesn't care about high scores, and neither should you. You can focus on teaching your dog agility and can put together simple courses. And handle your dog without stress. Get your friends involved, throw a party, and have fun running courses.

The courses in this book aren't likely to be found anywhere else. They're designed to provide a good time for both owners and dogs, without pressure. If you want some sort of real competition, there are matches and trials nearly every weekend all over the country. Any healthy dog of any age can do something in agility provided you take appropriate precautions, and mixed breeds are most certainly allowed.

Almost everyone starts in agility because it's fun. But if your dog turns out to be an athlete who loves to do it, competition may be a logical next step. This book will give you a taste of agility in a relaxed environment so that you can go on to more serious agility training discussed in books such as my *Introduction to Dog Agility*, *All about Agility* by Jacqueline O'Neil, or *Agility Training: The Fun Sport for All Dogs* by Jane Simons-Moake.

It's time to get started!

# Part One

# Learning Agility

# 1
# Getting Started

You've decided you want to try agility, but you're not sure how to get started. That's okay. In this chapter I'll help you decide if agility is the right activity for you and your dog. We'll go over your dog's basic fitness level, training, and age, as well as diet and exercise. In addition, we'll discuss your fitness level (don't worry!), what clothes will work for doing agility, and equipment requirements and training.

## Deciding If Agility Is Right for You and Your Dog

You may be wondering if agility is something you'd like to commit to doing with your dog. Drop by a fun match or even an agility trial and watch what goes on. (Be aware that you may be watching competition, which is something I don't cover in this book. If you're interested in getting started in competition, check out the agility books in the reference list at the back of this book.)

Unless you're planning on participating, don't bring your dog just yet. Watch the dogs as they go through the course. Notice the teamwork between the handler and her dog. Both members of this partnership have a special bond of trust in each other.

*Dogs love agility. This is JD, an Australian Shepherd owned by Margaret Meleski, performing the weave poles.*

"My dog can't do that!" you might say. "Look at all the work that went into training!" Yes, while training is part of agility, it's not as hard as you think nor is it harsh or rigorous. The agility training in this book uses only positive methods that are fun for you and your dog.

So let's look at possible reasons why you might think agility isn't right for you:

- *My dog is a mixed breed.* Fact: Mixed breeds do very well in agility and all sanctioning organizations allow mixed breeds in competition, except AKC.

- *I've never trained my dog to do anything before.* Fact: It's never too late to train a dog to do fun things.

## When Can I Start My Puppy in Agility?

Wait until your puppy is about six months old before starting him in agility. There are a number of good reasons for this. First, he'll need to complete all his vaccinations to ensure that he's protected against deadly diseases like parvovirus and distemper. Second, your puppy needs six months for his muscles and tendons to strengthen, and to gain coordination. Your puppy risks serious injury if he jumps higher than his hock height before he is fully grown. Check with your veterinarian before starting your puppy on an agility training program.

- *My dog could never do that.* Fact: Unless your dog is older than eight years old, has hip dysplasia, or is incapacitated in some way, he can do agility. Don't limit your dog by your preconceived notions. Even dogs older than eight can do agility in a limited fashion if they are in good health.

- *My dog is too small (or too large) for agility.* Fact: Toy breeds and giant breeds all compete in agility. I've seen Chihuahuas, Great Danes, and Basset Hounds do agility successfully.

- *I don't have time to do anything with my dog.* Fact: Why do you have a dog in the first place? A dog is a commitment and a companion, not an animal to be relegated to the backyard. If you have a dog, part of that commitment is to exercise her.

- *Agility equipment costs too much.* Fact: You can put together some agility equipment with just basic hand tools, and you can purchase some very inexpensive pieces as well. Agility clubs and training centers often have drop-in classes that allow your dog to train on equipment for a few bucks.

- *I don't know where I could go to learn agility.* Fact: There are agility trainers, classes, and clubs throughout the United States including Alaska, Montana, and Hawaii. Internationally, there are clubs in Argentina, Australia, Belgium, Bermuda, Canada, Columbia, Croatia, England, Finland, France, Germany, Hungary, Iceland, Italy, Japan, Mexico, Netherlands, New Zealand, Peru, Portugal, Scotland, South Africa, Spain, Sweden, and Switzerland, and more appear every day. If there isn't a club nearby, you can always get information, equipment, and support on the Internet.

- *I have a disability.* Fact: Many people with disabilities have trained and competed in agility. Since you're considering agility for fun and not for competition, this is a great way to interact with your dog.

### My Newest Agility Dog

Sometimes choosing an agility dog is easy. Haegl, my youngest Malamute, climbs along the back of the couch and walks the edge like a circus acrobat. He opens crate doors to get at toys and closes them again. After a snowstorm, I caught him climbing the ladder that led to the roof (the snow had stabilized the ladder). One day, he leapt straight up on top of a crate. He became the obvious choice for my agility dog when Kiana passed on.

- *I'm out of shape (or overweight, or older, or can't run a lot).* Fact: While competitive teams may run around, agility is something you can do at your own pace and at your leisure. Some people who can't run much have taught their dogs to run the course without them by directing the dog toward the obstacles.

There are some legitimate reasons for not trying agility. These include:

- Your dog is too old and feeble or has an injury or medical condition that precludes him from doing agility without getting injured or harming his health.
- Your dog is aggressive toward people or other dogs. Work out the behavioral problems with an animal behaviorist before exposing your pet to others.
- Your dog is too young. Wait until your puppy is about six months old before starting agility. Then jump him only at heights below his hock and take extra precautions so he doesn't risk injury before he's fully grown.

## Your Dog

Before you get started in agility, you need to evaluate your dog. If you have one dog, she is going to be your agility dog. If you have more than one dog, you can try doing agility with all of them, but it's better if you select one and focus on her. No doubt you have a favorite dog among your gang or an idea of which dog would make the ideal agility dog. Trust your instincts because part of agility is that special bond between you and your pet. You can train the other dogs after you've had some success with your first agility dog.

## Examining Your Dog

Before you get started in agility, your dog should be healthy and free from injuries and limps. Look at your dog as if seeing her for the first time and watch how she moves. Is she slow and glitchy or fast and fluid? Does she like chasing a tennis ball or prefer napping by the fire? Did she climb on the bed when young, but doesn't now? Watch for a hitch in her movement—a limp or perhaps a favoring to one side or the other. Some limps are subtle and hard for an owner to detect, so watch her carefully.

You can do a quick examination to determine the health of your dog. Look for anything abnormal; an underlying illness should be remedied before doing agility.

- Ears—should be clean and sweet smelling. Any foul odor or excessive buildup of wax indicates a potential ear problem.
- Eyes—should be clear and bright without excessive or puslike discharge. No redness or tearing.
- Legs—feel your dog's legs to check for any lumps or bumps. Inspect the footpads for cuts and foreign objects such as foxtails. Look at the toenails; they shouldn't be red or broken. If you find an unusual bump, check the other side to see if it is normal. If the bump is unilateral, then it might be a tumor. Check the legs for full range of motion, moving them slowly and gently. There should be no clicks or pops.

### Mixed Breeds Allowed

Mixed breeds are encouraged in agility. In all forms of agility, except those run by the American Kennel Club, mixed breeds are allowed to participate. They do just as well as purebred dogs. The only advantage an AKC-registered, purebred dog has is that he can earn AKC titles. Mixed breeds earn their titles from other agility organizations.

- Reproductive organs—there should not be a discharge from the vagina or penis (except in intact female dogs where discharge is normal during estrus).
- Skin and fur—the skin should be free of any sores, bald patches, or redness and should not be dry or flaky. Are there dark grains through the fur that turn red when wet? This is a sign of fleas.
- Mouth—teeth should be white and clean, without a tartar buildup. Your dog's breath should not be foul smelling; if it is, it may suggest tooth or gum problems. Are the gums a healthy pink or are they red?
- Nose—should be cool to touch and moist. Hot and dry may indicate a fever. There should be no discharge or blood.
- Tail—should be healthy looking, not hanging limp. There may be a problem if your dog has been chewing on it.

Look at your dog's appetite and attitude. She should be happy, energetic, and eating well. Signs of illness or injury may include:

- Lack of appetite
- Diarrhea, vomiting, or dehydration
- Limping or swollen limbs
- Tenderness in a particular area or an area that is hot to the touch
- Bleeding or discharge; a wound or cut skin
- Unusual discharge coming from the nose, the eyes, the mouth, the anus, or the sexual organs
- Abnormal lumps or bumps
- Red, itchy skin; hair loss
- Red, swollen gums; bad breath; broken teeth
- Fever (temperature over 102.5°F)
- Unexplained tiredness, or listlessness
- Inability or reluctance to do things she used to do

## Sometimes It's Not Obvious

Conan had been doing agility for a short while before we stopped. Something didn't seem right. He was an older Newfoundland-Samoyed mix with a funny gait. He had always had that funny gait and I never thought much of it because he was so enthusiastic. One day, when I was having him examined for a knee problem, my veterinarian made a casual remark about his elbow dysplasia.

I was stunned. Elbow dysplasia? I looked at Conan again, and sure enough, he had the signs: elbows that stuck out at the sides and a funny stance. With any other dog, it would've been obvious to me. I just never saw it because he had always had it and never showed any discomfort.

# Visiting the Veterinarian

Before you start any training program, you should have your veterinarian examine your dog for potential health problems. He should check for joint problems, including congenital and hereditary hip and elbow dysplasia. Even if your dog is a mixed breed, he can still get hereditary hip dysplasia.

The only way to determine if your dog has hip dysplasia is through an X-ray at two or more years old. However, you can have preliminary X-rays done to determine if there might be a potential problem. Other problems to consider are joint malformations and arthritis.

Your vet may also be able to detect some forms of heart abnormalities and other conditions that would preclude your dog from doing strenuous exercise. Finally, he should evaluate your dog's weight to determine if she is too heavy for agility. Excessive weight will stress joints, which will cause injuries.

You may have to guide your veterinarian in what you're looking for. Discuss what activities you're going to do with your dog and ask him to look for anything unusual. Sometimes your vet can catch a problem you might not. If you have particular concerns, talk them over with your vet now. For example, if Shadow usually climbs on the couch but now refuses to hop up when you invite her, it may be a sign of arthritis or injury. Your vet may recommend a regiment of rest and maybe some medications or nutritional supplements that will help your dog regain or add flexibility.

## Fitness Level

Which brings us to your dog's fitness level. Although you're planning on doing agility for fun, your dog will need to be at the right weight and conditioning or he may injure himself. As I said earlier, if your dog is too heavy, his weight will put stress on his joints. But weight is not the only factor. Your dog should start a light exercise program to stretch and work his muscles and joints to avoid strain. Walking, playing ball, and other activities may be all that your dog needs before starting in agility.

Your veterinarian should examine your dog before your dog begins an exercise program. Be aware that your vet often sees couch-potato house pets (not athletes) and may erroneously think your dog is fit. A dog's weight is a good baseline for comparing her to the breed standard, but it isn't a good measure of your dog's fitness. Body structure varies from dog to dog, even within a breed, so weight is, at best, a rough guideline.

The easiest way to determine if your dog is fat is to look at your dog's shape. There should be a tuck where your dog's abdomen (waist) is, both in profile and looking from above. Place your thumbs on your dog's spine and feel her ribs. If you have an "amazing ribless dog" or if you can barely feel her ribs through the heavy padding, she is obese and needs to shed some pounds. You should also be able to feel your dog's hip bones and spine.

Sometimes cutting back on treats or switching to lower calorie food and snacks is all you need to do. But if your dog is truly obese and you're feeding her a bit less than the amount recommended on the package, talk with your vet. The problem might be medical, such as thyroid. Even if it's not, your vet can help you put your dog on a diet. There are specially formulated prescription diets that work well.

### Fun Activities to Get Your Dog in Shape

- Long walks or hikes
- Running beside you on a bicycle
- Playing fetch
- Chasing a flying disc

## Basics in the Home

"Watch me," "sit," "come," "down," and "stay" are commands your dog needs to know. If you haven't taught him the basics, start now. Chapter 2 covers how to teach "sit," "down," and a version of "come" called "here." You can teach these commands with positive reinforcement or clicker training.

As you begin teaching the basics and work in agility, your dog will become more fun to be around. A couple of other basic commands are included here.

*Watch me* can be done with or without a clicker. Say "Watch me!" and bring a piece of food to the bridge of your nose. When your dog makes eye contact, drop the food and praise him (or click and treat). Do this several times and your dog will be watching you in no time.

*"Stay"* is just an extension of "sit" or "down." When your dog is in the sit or down position, lengthen the time before you release him by saying "stay" and holding your hand out, palm down and flat. Wait a few moments and then release your dog with "okay." If your dog doesn't hold his stay, put him back into his stay and give him a few more seconds before releasing him and giving the treat. Gradually work your way up to five seconds or more.

## Warming Up/Cooling Down

Before you begin exercising your dog, you'll need to learn how to warm up your dog and let her cool down, just as you would an athlete. Warming up allows the dog's muscles to become more flexible and less prone to tears and injury. Cooling down helps remove the lactic acid from the muscles and helps prevent soreness and stiffness the next day.

You can warm up your dog by walking her slowly at first and gradually increasing her speed to a slow trot for about ten minutes. Then, after she has been warmed up, you can help her stretch. If you've never helped your dog stretch, it might be a good idea to ask an experienced person to show you. Always follow these guidelines when helping your dog stretch:

- Any movement must be gentle, slow, and not forced.
- Only stretch the body in a position that's natural to your dog. Anything else could cause serious injury.
- If your dog shows pain at any time or if the stretch looks uncomfortable, stop immediately.

When you stretch your dog's legs, you must mimic the natural motion of the leg; namely, if the leg doesn't bend that way normally, you shouldn't do it. You'll work from front to back. Stand beside your dog next to the leg you're going to stretch and face the same direction as your dog. Support your dog's elbow underneath and hold your dog's front leg. Push gently upward on the elbow. Stretch the leg to its full extension so that you hold his leg in front. Then, put your hand on the front of his shoulder blade and bring the leg backward so that he has a slow stretch in the opposite direction. Release. Do this a few times. Then, work the opposite front leg.

Once you've stretched your dog's front legs, go to the back legs. Stand facing the opposite direction from your dog. Take one of the back legs and use your hand to support your dog's knee. Push gently on the hip so that your dog's leg flexes backward. Now, put your hand on your dog's rear and move the leg so that it is in a natural forward position. Don't force it; it won't have quite the same flexibility. Hold the leg and then release. Do this a few times and then work the opposite back leg. Once you have stretched your dog's legs, take her for a slow trot for a minute or so.

*Stretch her leg out gently. This is the author's Alaskan Malamute Kira, or Belle's Kira of Sky Warrior.*

*While holding her leg against her chest, push on her shoulders gently.*

*Kira patiently enjoys a good warm-up. Bring her leg back for a nice stretch.
Don't force it.*

After exercising, your dog will need to cool down. Take her for a brisk walk and gradually slow it so that she's walking at a leisurely pace. The cool-down can take from five to ten minutes, depending on how hard she was working.

## Preparing Yourself for Agility

Now you know how to prepare your dog, but what about you? While you don't have to be in athletic shape, it doesn't hurt if you're fit. Still, many agility competitors are overweight, have knee or other joint problems, or aren't very active.

*Did someone say "teeter?" Gideon is very serious about the seesaw. He is a Brussels Griffon owned by Joyce Tessier.*

---

### Books with Agility Equipment Plans

*Do-It-Yourself Agility Equipment: Constructing Agility Equipment for Training or Competition* by Jim Hutchins (Clean Run Productions, 2002) www.cleanrun.com.

*Introduction to Dog Agility* by Margaret H. Bonham (Barron's Educational Series, 2000).

*Agility Training: The Fun Sport for All Dogs* by Jane Simmons-Moake (Howell Book House, 1992).

---

## Exercise

If you're not used to physical activity, you might want to start a walking program or something that gives you some exercise at least three times a week. (Caveat: Before beginning any exercise program, consult with your doctor first.) Even a light walking program will help improve your cardiovascular system. If you're physically active, doing agility shouldn't be difficult. If you have a disability, consult with your doctor for the best exercises for your situation.

## Clothing

Dressing for agility is simply wearing the most comfortable clothing for movement. If a T-shirt and jeans are the most comfortable, wear them!

One caveat is footwear. You need to wear sneakers with good treads and proper support. It doesn't matter whether they're for cross-training, running, or walking. If you have ankle problems (like I do) you may want a sneaker specially designed to support the ankle and prevent it from rolling. I have a tall pair of light hiking boots (similar to sneakers) that I wear all the time, especially for agility. This way, I won't accidentally turn an ankle while running a course.

# Equipment

So, now you know the basics for getting you and your dog ready. But what about agility equipment? Agility equipment is very bulky and can be expensive, so before you commit to building or buying

*The tire is a fun obstacle. This is Demi, owned by Jeanne S. Grim, D.V.M.*

*Flying across a dog walk with confidence. This is Sableman, a Cocker Spaniel owned by Pam Metzger.*

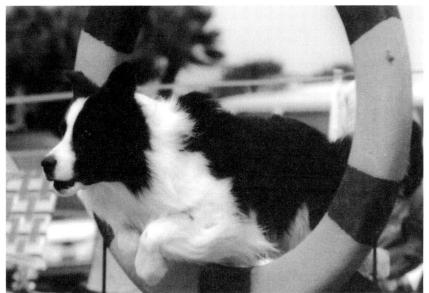

*Through the tire and on to the next obstacle. This is Rush, a Border Collie owned by Lisa Dewey.*

anything, you may want to try agility first. Most training facilities and agility clubs have drop-in days when you can try out agility and see if this is something for you. You may wish to take a basic agility class as well to become familiar with the obstacles in a controlled environment.

## Building Your Own

If you're handy or if you have a friend, spouse, or relative who can build agility equipment for you, consider yourself lucky. There are many good plans for building agility equipment, including some low-cost options. See the sidebar for books on agility equipment.

## Buying

Another option for obtaining agility equipment is to buy it. This is usually much more expensive than building your own; however, if you're not handy and you make frequent trips to the emergency room after your spouse picks up a hammer, then this is your only option.

*Mutts like Robyn excel in agility. She is owned by Jim and Kathy Stabler.*

If you can find someone local who builds and sells agility equipment, sometimes you can get a discount if you buy more than one piece. Or you can ask around to see if anyone is getting out of agility or upgrading and would like to sell their equipment. You can sometimes get a good deal there. Looking on ebay.com or searching the Internet is another way to find low-cost equipment.

## Summary

- Agility is great fun for you and your dog.
- Agility isn't right for dogs who have severe joint problems, are too young, or have medical conditions that would preclude doing agility in a safe manner.
- Agility is an international activity with clubs or training facilities in all fifty states and over twenty countries.
- Before beginning any exercise activity, have your veterinarian examine your dog for potential health problems.
- If your dog is overweight, you may have to put him on a diet and exercise program. Your veterinarian can help.

## Agility Equipment on the Web

The following are agility equipment suppliers on the Web. This list is not all-inclusive nor do I endorse any of these suppliers. They are here simply for informational purposes:

Affordable Agility—http://www.affordableagility.com

Agility Ability—http://www.agilityability.com

Agility for Less—http://www.agilityforless.com

Champion Tunnels—http://www.championtunnels.com

Dog Equipment.com—http://www.dogequipment.com

eBay—http://www.ebay.com

J and J Dog Supply—http://www.jjdog.com

Max 200—http://www.max200.com

Northwest Agility Products—http://www.nwagility.com

Weave Poles.com—http://www.weave-poles.com

- Know how to warm up and stretch your dog to prevent injury. A cool-down period will help your dog's body remove lactic acid in your dog's muscles.
- You may want to increase your own exercise before starting agility. Go slow and consult a doctor before starting any exercise program.
- You can wear anything you like for agility as long as it's comfortable. Wear sneakers with good treads when doing agility.
- Decide whether agility is a good activity for you and your dog before committing to the expense of buying or building equipment.

# 2

# Clicker for Fun (Learning the Rules)

Are you ready to play games? Playing games is fun, but your dog has to know the rules. Think back to some of the games you and your dog played in the past; almost all the fun ones have a set of rules. Playing games in agility has some rules too, even though they're relaxed.

How do you teach your dog these rules? What may appear to be logical to you is baffling to your canine companion. ("You want me to do *what*?") Dogs don't think like humans, and in the translation from human to canine the finer points get lost. You may see the pipe tunnel as being simple and easy (and to dogs familiar with the tunnel, it *is*), but to a beginning agility star, it can look pretty scary. "You want me to go in there? No way!" your dog may be thinking. "It looks like it might swallow me whole!"

One way to instill confidence in any canine is to teach him something. Think about the things you learned that mattered to you and made you more confident. They weren't easy to do, were they? It is the same with dogs. Dogs love a challenge or they get bored,

---

### Definitions

**operant conditioning**—A learning method where the animal learns according to his actions.

**positive reinforcement**—A training method where you reward desirable behavior.

**negative reinforcement**—A training method where you punish or discourage an undesirable behavior.

---

and that's no fun. So, let's teach your dog some easy commands that will allow him to play by the rules.

Commands? You may be wondering if this is obedience. Well, not exactly. You may have seen obedience where the dogs are required to sit precisely, come in a straight line, and heel perfectly. You can most certainly do that if you want to, but there's no need for that here. You won't need choke chains or coercive techniques. In this chapter, I'll explain how to train with or without the clicker using positive techniques.

## What Is Clicker Training?

If you've never trained with a clicker, you're in for a treat. It's so much fun for both you and your dog that I guarantee it won't feel like training. Clicker training is a form of *operant conditioning*, meaning that the dog learns something according to his actions. Operant conditioning is how most animals learn (even people!). On the

---

### Tools of the Trade

You'll need the following:

- Clicker
- Target stick
- Six-foot leather leash
- Six-inch tab
- Retractable lead (Flexi-lead) or tracking lead
- Treat bag

---

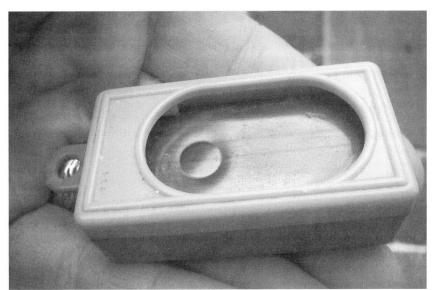

*The clicker fits in the palm of your hand.*

*Press down on the black metal to click.*

## You Can't Make a 120-pound Malamute Do Anything He Doesn't Want to Do

If a big dog doesn't want to do something, he generally won't. That's the lesson I learned with big male Malamutes. They're far stronger and more stubborn than I'll ever be. I originally learned how to train dogs under the old coercive methods. While they're effective to a point, it's easier to get dogs to do what you want by providing rewards. This is important with big dogs who can out-muscle you in most circumstances.

I started training Haegl with a clicker when he was very young. In no time, he learned to speak, wave, shake hands, close doors (and figured out how to open doors), and pick up my keys.

positive reinforcement side of operant conditioning, the animal does something desirable and receives a reward. (This works with negative reinforcement as well. The animal does something undesirable and receives a punishment.)

Clicker training uses primarily positive reinforcement, i.e., the animal does something and receives a reward. With the clicker, you teach your dog to associate the sound of the click with a treat. When your dog does something right, you click and treat. When he performs a behavior you don't want, you ignore it. Sounds pretty simple, doesn't it?

Clicking works much the same as praise does, although instead of saying "good dog!" you click. Click; treat. It's very simple. Your dog will associate the correct action (the one you clicked for) with the treat.

## Teaching the Clicker

So, how do you get started? First, you must have the proper tools: a clicker, a target stick, and a treat your dog really loves. This treat should be cut into small portions so that you can give him a lot

### Click Trick

Your dog will understand clicker training even faster if you click and put down his bowl of food at mealtime.

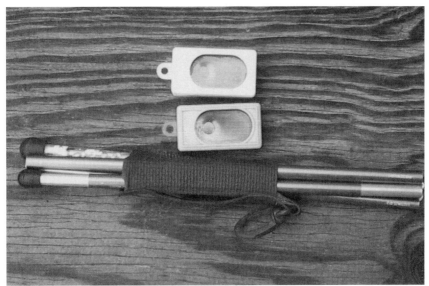

*Two different clickers and a fold-up target stick.*

without getting him fat, ruining his appetite, or upsetting his digestive system. Many people use diced cold cuts, hot dogs, or cheese, but you can try other favorites as well. Just be sure to cut them into tiny portions because you're going to be feeding him a lot of these.

## Lesson One: Introduction to the Clicker

Start before your dog's feeding time, when he's a bit hungry. Show him the clicker. Now, click and give him a treat. If your dog is startled by the loud noise, try muffling it a bit in your hand when you click it.

Click and give him a treat. Click, treat. Click, treat. You may have to do this for a bit, but at some point, your dog will start realizing that when he hears a click he's going to get a treat. When you click, he should look expectantly at you for the treat.

Sometimes it takes a while for the dog to make the association. This is okay. If, after five minutes or so, you haven't made any

### Click Trick

Spend no more than five to ten minutes a day training with the clicker. When you're done, play with your dog to reward her for her hard work!

## Where to Purchase Clicker Equipment

Many training facilities and even pet supply stores have clickers, but you can also purchase them online from Karen Pryor's Web site at www.clickertraining.com or by calling 1-800-47-CLICK. You can purchase a target stick there, too; or, if you want to make your own target stick, buy a yard-long 1/4-inch dowel and either paint it or cover it with colorful tape.

progress, put away the clicker and play with your dog. Try again tomorrow. At some point, your dog is going to make the association between the click and the treat. When he does, you'll be ready for lesson two.

## Lesson Two: Varying the Response Times

Once your dog has figured out that treats come with clicks, the next step is to vary the time between the click and the treat and where he receives the treat. This will teach your dog that she can expect a treat even if it's a little delayed or it may not be in your hand, but tossed on the ground. Remember that your dog must first associate the click with the treat before you proceed to this next step.

Click the clicker and silently count to five. Your dog may look expectantly to you or even drool a bit because she knows what's coming. Give her the treat. Now click again and count to three silently and then treat her. Now click and silently count to ten and then treat. If she gets insistent or pushy, don't do anything. Just wait until she stops before you give her the treat. Her correct response is to wait patiently before getting the treat.

## Click Trick

You may be wondering if you *have* to use a clicker. The answer is no. The clicker serves as a marker, that is, a unique sound that lets the dog know the moment the behavior is done right. You can substitute other sounds (whistle, tongue click, or even a "good boy!") but be certain that they're definite and you can time them with the behavior. Clickers are useful because they're distinct and a dog recognizes the sound.

## Click Trick

If you have multiple dogs, train only one dog at a time with the clicker; otherwise, you'll confuse matters. Choose a special place away from the others so that you can train in peace. Dogs love clicker training so much, they'll howl for it!

Once your dog is used to varying times, click and toss the treat in front of her. Your dog should eat the treat, but if she has problems, show her the treat and tell her "good dog!" when she picks it up. Click the clicker and toss the treat somewhere else once she has figured out that the treat doesn't have to come from your hand.

## Lesson Three: Training with the Target Stick

Once your dog is used to hearing a click and receiving a treat, now the fun begins! Start with target stick training. Target sticks are great for teaching your dog where to go or to touch certain things with his nose or paw.

*The author's Alaskan Malamute, Haegl (Belle's Lachlans Black Dragon), demonstrating the "touch it" command while barking (yes, he is enthusiastic!).*

First, get out your clicker, the bags of treats, and the target stick. Hold the target stick out for your dog to sniff. If he touches the stick, click and treat. You may have to wiggle the stick a bit to get him interested in it. Even if he accidentally touches it, you must click and treat.

Suppose your dog doesn't touch the stick? Well, you can try shaping the behavior. *Shaping* is a fancy term for teaching the behavior you want in small increments. For example, you will click and treat when your dog *looks* at the stick. Every time your dog looks at the stick, you should click and treat. Then, after he looks at the stick and waits for you to click, wait and see what he does next. Your dog may stare at it longer or perhaps nudge or paw the stick. If he needs encouragement, wave the stick close to him, but don't touch the stick to him; instead, let your dog touch the stick. Then click and treat.

Once your dog touches the stick and subsequently hears a click and gets a treat, he may be puzzled. After all, he's been doing nothing to get a click and treat, but now he has to work for it. Offer the stick again and see if your dog will touch it (accidentally or on purpose). Click and treat when he does.

Some dogs learn touching the target stick quickly. Others take time and you may have to have several sessions. Once your dog touches the target stick consistently, start using a cue word, such as "touch."

## Lesson Four: Adding Commands or Cue Words

In lesson three, you used the cue word "touch." Although we tend to call such words "commands," these words are actually cues for the behavior you want your dog to do. Your dog may already know some cue words, such as "sit," "down," or "come."

---

### Definitions

**shaping**—Starting with a basic behavior that is relatively easy to obtain and slowly progressing in increments to obtain the behavior that you want. For example, teaching a dog to touch something with his paw can be shaped to waving good-bye, closing or opening a door, or other behaviors by clicking at incremental steps until the dog displays the final desired behavior.

---

## Click Trick

Learning "touch," "paw it," and "nose it" are very important when training a dog with a clicker. You can use the target stick to move your dog where you need her without pushing and pulling.

Once your dog knows "touch," you can begin to differentiate between touching the target stick with the nose ("nose it") and touching it with the paw ("paw it"). Make it easy for your dog by putting the target stick close to either his nose or his paw. To work on "paw it," wait for her to touch it appropriately. Click and treat. She should start pawing the target stick. Click and treat each time. Now that she's primed for pawing the target stick, say "paw it" before she paws it and click and treat. Add this cue word and move the stick around so she has to work a bit to touch it with her paw. Give her the command "paw it" each time and click and treat.

You need to teach her "nose it" as well. Teach your dog the same way you taught "paw it," only click and treat when she puts her nose on the touch stick.

# Should You Train with a Clicker or Use Other Positive Reinforcement Techniques?

Now that you've learned a bit about clicker training, you might be surprised to hear that it's not for every dog or trainer. Almost all dogs respond in some way to positive reinforcement, but there's no way to gauge whether you'll be successful training with a clicker or another positive technique. Regardless of whether you decide to teach your dog using a clicker or some other method, be certain that it is always positive and not coercive in any way. You're teaching your dog to have fun, not forcing him to do something he doesn't want to do.

The following instructions include clicker and another method of positive training. There are two types of clicker training. The first is where you wait for the behavior to appear, i.e., wait until your dog lies down, and then click for it. This can be time consuming and very difficult if your dog doesn't exhibit the behavior often. You are certainly welcome to try that if you have the time and patience. Otherwise, I'll

## Click Trick

### *Fading the Lure or Target Stick*

When you first teach a particular trick or command, you may need to use a lure (such as a treat) or the target stick to get your dog to do what you'd like. However, you may not want to always use a lure or target stick. The concept is called *fading*, meaning that you slowly remove the lure or the target stick from use.

For example, let's say you originally used the target stick to teach her to sit by following the stick backward. You fade the command for the target stick by first dropping the "nose it" command. Then, you fade the stick by holding it so that your hand covers the end as you move it over her head and emphasize the "sit" command. Then, remove the stick and simply use a hand gesture instead of bringing the target stick over her nose. Slowly reduce the hand gesture until you stop using the gesture altogether.

offer a speedier version. I also offer the positive training method of teaching the dog commands. Again, different dogs learn differently and there are many good positive techniques. While training, put a flat collar on your dog snug enough so he can't pull out. Clip his leash to his collar so that he stays with you and doesn't wander. Finally, train in an enclosed area with few or no distractions so that your dog will focus on you and not on the neighbor's cat or the kids playing softball next door or a thousand other fun things. What you're doing is fun too, but it needs full attention from your dog.

When you start training commands, remember that sometimes it's very difficult for a dog to understand what you're trying to teach him. Be patient. If at any time the training is going badly, stop and have your dog do something he knows how to do, so you can praise him. Then end your training with a play session.

## Sit

"Sit" is a useful command, both for agility and everyday manners. There will be many times when knowing "sit" will be useful as a means of controlling your dog.

## ✓ Clicker Method

Take a treat or use the target stick and hold it over your dog's nose. Tell your dog to "nose it" and bring the treat or target stick backward. As she follows the treat or the target stick, her rump will start to drop. Most dogs will fold naturally into a sit. When her rump touches the floor, click and treat. Repeat several times.

For a dog who does not naturally sit, or backs up instead of sitting, try teaching her to sit with her back to the wall so that she must sit because she doesn't have anywhere to go.

Once you have your dog sitting with the clicker, add the command. Tell her "sit!" Once your dog is familiar with the command, you'll need to fade the lure or target stick. Instead, substitute the command.

## ★ Positive Method

Take a treat and hold it over your dog's nose. Move the treat backward while gently pushing on your dog's rear end. Tell her "Shadow, sit!" Give her the treat and praise her once she sits. Some dogs may not naturally sit. If she won't sit or if she backs up instead of sitting, try teaching her to sit with her back to the wall so that she must sit because she doesn't have anywhere to go. Practice this a few times until she starts sitting on command.

# Down

"Down" is also a useful command, both for agility and everyday manners. In competition agility, dogs may be required to do a down and hold it for five seconds. Even outside competition agility, knowing "down" is useful as there are times when your dog needs to lie down.

## ✓ Clicker Method

Have your dog sit. Take a treat or use the target stick and hold it below your dog's nose. Tell your dog to "nose it" and bring the treat or target stick downward toward her chest. As she follows the treat or the target stick, her front legs will start to drop. When her elbows touch the floor, click and treat. Repeat several times.

Once your dog lies down with the clicker, add the command "down!" Once your dog is familiar with the command, you'll need to fade the lure or target stick. Instead, substitute the command to lie down.

## ★ Positive Method

Have your dog sit. Take a treat and hold it below your dog's nose. Bring the treat downward toward her chest while gently pushing on your dog's shoulders. Tell her "Shadow, down!" Give her the treat and praise her once she lies down. Practice this a few times until she starts lying down on command.

# Here

The "here" command is a lot like the "come" command, only it's less stringent. "Here" means "come toward me" but doesn't require your dog to come right to you. This command is important in agility when you're trying to call your dog away from the wrong obstacle or if you want your dog to run closer by your side.

An important aspect to training "here" is to always reward your dog for coming to you. That means that if you have to correct your dog, you should go to him, *not* call him to you. The second part to training "here" is to do so in an enclosed area. This is very important if your dog sees something he'd rather chase. If you're unable to train in an enclosed area, an alternative is using a retractable leash (Flexi-lead) or tracking lead.

## ✓ Clicker Method

Let your dog loose in an enclosed area. Most dogs, when they know you have treats, will come right to you. Click and treat. If your dog

### Haegl and the Clicker

Bringing out the clicker causes a great stir at my house. Haegl and the other dogs know it's time to train. Haegl will begin to woof or perhaps wave his paw to see if I will click and treat him for it. It's fun to see a dog get so enthusiastic over something this simple.

## Click Trick

### Finding a Motivational Object

Most of positive reinforcement training (and clicker training) requires a motivational object. This is usually some type of food your dog is wild about, but it doesn't have to be. Some people use a toy or something that excites the dog. I've seen dogs go wild over tennis balls, rabbit skins, cat toys on a fishing pole, pine cones, Frisbees, soap bubbles, light dots from laser pointers, and other silly things. When people tell me that their dogs aren't motivated, I usually suggest that they try other foods and toys. Something is bound to get your dog's attention.

doesn't come to you while loose, try showing him the treat and click and treat when he comes.

Once he comes to you, start using the cue word "here!" You can pair it with your dog's name, such as, "Shadow, here!" and click and treat. Remember, you want him to come to you, but it's not required that he stays with you.

## ★ Positive Method

Let your dog loose in an enclosed area. Most dogs, when they know you have treats, will come right to you. Show him the treat and call him over in a happy voice "Shadow, here!" Praise him and give him the treat when he comes. Let him leave if he wishes and then call him back to you. Remember, you want him to come to you, but it's not required that he stays with you.

## Go Out

"Go out" is a difficult concept for most dogs to master. It's relatively easy to get them to come to you, but harder to send them away from you. And yet, it's a command you'll need when training in agility. Your dog must leave your side to go into the tunnel or to go to another obstacle.

The training largely depends on whether your dog is food oriented or has a favorite toy. If your dog loves food, tossing a favorite treat away from you will be the reward when your dog leaves your

---

### Using Hand Signals

It's okay to use hand signals to reinforce what you want in agility. In fact, even in competitive agility, it's perfectly acceptable. The hand signals reinforce what you're trying to communicate.

---

side. If your dog has a favorite toy, you can use that to convince him to go out. If your dog is independent, you may have a hard time calling him back.

Regardless whether your dog is food- or toy-oriented, always train in an enclosed area or keep your dog on a retractable or long lead while teaching him this command. Otherwise, you may have a hard time rounding him up.

## ✔ Clicker Method

Start by throwing the treat or toy a small distance away from you. As your dog turns toward the treat, click and let him pick up the treat or toy. Call him with a "here" command and click and treat. Then, toss a treat or toy away again. When he goes to get it, click before he eats the treat. Repeat until he has an idea that he needs to move away from you.

Now add the cue words "go out!" and toss the treat. Click as he goes away from you. As you associate the command with going away from you, tell your dog to "go out" and wait for a moment. If he knows the cue words, he'll start to move away. Click now and then toss the treat. You'll want to expand the time between the cue and the click so that your dog will go out farther each time.

## ★ Positive Method

Start by throwing the treat or toy a small distance away from you. As your dog turns toward the treat, give him the command, "go out!" After he picks up the treat or toy, call him back with a "here!" and offer another treat when he comes back. Then, toss a treat or toy away again. When he goes to get it, give him the command "go out!" again.

As you associate the command with going away from you, tell your dog to "go out" and wait for a moment. If he knows the command, he'll start to move away. Now toss the treat. You'll want to expand the time between the command and the treat so that your dog will go out farther each time.

# Go Over (Hurdles)

Now we come to some agility work! You may be surprised to hear that learning to jump takes time and practice. Not all dogs are born with the knowledge of how to jump properly.

Don't initially set your hurdle to the highest bar and expect your dog to jump this. It may feel good to watch a little dog jump an enormous height, but it does nothing for your dog, expect perhaps overexert her. Start with the lowest possible jump height and work your way up slowly.

Use a plain hurdle without wings. Put away the broad jumps, tire hurdle, and double and triple jumps for now. You'll work on them later.

Before you begin jumping your dog, be sure that your vet has cleared her for hip dysplasia, elbow dysplasia, arthritis, and other joint problems. Even mixed breeds can get hip and elbow dysplasia.

## ✓ Clicker Method

Set up your hurdle, clip a leash on your dog's collar, and lead her over to the hurdle. Let your dog inspect it. Put the bar at the lowest height (4 to 8 inches, unless your dog is a toy, in which case, leave the bar on the ground). If your dog steps over the bar, click and treat. She may be surprised by this and try to step over it again. Click and treat.

---

### Jumping Precautions

Jumping is very stressful on a dog's joints. He should only jump at a height that is comfortable. Never allow a puppy younger than eighteen months to jump above his hock height. Before this time, a puppy's growth plates in his legs haven't closed. If you own a giant breed younger than two years, you may want to have your vet's advice on whether his growth plates have closed before you allow him to jump.

Choose a padded, even, nonslip surface to jump on. Carpeted areas, grassy areas, and horse arenas work well. Concrete is hard on a dog's joints and is too slick without some pads or nonskid mats.

---

## Jump Heights

Always start with a low jump height and work your way up slowly. Most dogs shouldn't jump any higher than their shoulder height.

To measure your dog's shoulder height, stand him beside a wall and lay a ruler flat at the top point of his shoulder blades, perpendicular to the floor. Mark the wall where the ruler touches and measure the height from the floor to the mark, minus the thickness of the ruler. Use this as a measuring guideline.

**Recommended Jump Heights**

| Breed Type | Shoulder Height | Jump Height |
|---|---|---|
| Toy | Less than 12 inches | 2–8 inches |
| Small | 12–14 inches | 8–12 inches |
| Medium | 14–17 inches | 12–16 inches |
| Large | 17–22 inches | 16–20 inches |
| Giant | 22 inches and over | 16–20 inches |

Note that these recommended jump heights are for dogs who are healthy and without joint problems. Dogs more than eight years old should jump lower heights (at least one size down or lower) and puppies should never jump higher than their hock height.

You can try leading your dog over the jump if she doesn't try to walk over it; however, you should not try to force her over if she is apprehensive about the hurdle. If she is, try removing her leash and clicking and treating when she looks at the hurdle or expresses any interest in it. Once she shows enough interest, you can try luring her over the hurdle; click and treat once she steps over it.

Once you get your dog to readily go over the hurdle for a click and treat, add a cue such as "go over," "jump," or "hup." Continue to click and treat as she jumps over the hurdle.

Once she learns the cue word, you can then increase the height of the jump, *by one notch.* Work at this height until she gets comfortable with it before increasing to the next level.

## ★ Positive Method

Set up your hurdle, clip a leash on your dog's collar, and lead her over to the hurdle. Let your dog inspect it. Put the bar at the lowest height (4 to 8 inches, unless your dog is a toy, in which case, leave the bar on the ground). If your dog steps over the bar, praise her and give her a treat. She may be surprised by this and try to step over it again. Praise her again and give her a treat.

You can try leading your dog over the jump if she doesn't try to walk over it; however, you should not try to force her over if she is apprehensive about the hurdle. If she is, try luring her over the hurdle and treating once she steps over it. Sometimes clipping a leash on her collar and having her focus on the treat, while running her quickly over the hurdle is all that is needed. Give her the treat and praise when she jumps over it. Use the command "go over," "jump," or "hup" to associate the command with jumping.

Once she learns the command and jumps over the hurdle with ease, you can then increase the height of the jump, *by one notch*. Work at this height until she gets comfortable with it before increasing to the next level.

## Follow My Hands

"Follow my hands" is both appropriate for clicker and positive reinforcement methods. Take a favorite treat in each hand and show one to your dog. Let him follow the treat as you move your hand and give him the treat when he touches your hand. Then show him your other hand and let him follow that. Each time he follows your hand successfully, give him praise (or a click) and the treat.

## Go Right or Left

Once your dog learns how to jump, it's time to teach him right from left. This may sound like a circus trick instead of something you'd teach in agility, but it's important to teach so you can tell your dog which obstacle to take, especially if you're planning on having two obstacles that are side-by-side (known as *traps* in the agility world)

### At What Height Should I Train?

Because jumping is very strenuous on the joints, you should train at lower heights and occasionally mix in your maximum height. This will help your dog work on accuracy at the higher heights.

*Demi, a Cocker Spaniel owned by Jeanne S. Grim, D.V.M., takes a jump.*

or more complex courses. Plus, imagine how surprised your friends will be when you tell your dog to go right or left and he does!

Line up two plain hurdles without wings so that they're side by side and make a straight line lengthwise so that your dog can choose either the one on the left or the one on the right. Keep the hurdles at the lowest height or lay the bars on the ground, if your dog is a toy breed. Use either your hands or the target stick to direct your dog over the hurdles.

## ✓ Clicker Method

Your dog should be loose for this exercise (be sure to have him in an enclosed area). Put your dog in a sit and direct him over the right-hand jump with the target stick or your hand and use the words "touch! over!" If he's familiar with the target stick, he'll head for the target stick and go over the jump. Click and treat.

If adding the target stick and the jump is confusing to him, work with him on touching the target stick near the jump. Once he's touching the target stick, add the jump. You'll click first for the target stick touch and then click for the jump. Then, once he is going to the target stick and jumping, you can *chain* the two commands together and click just once. When he's mastered this, start substituting the word "right" for "touch." So, your dog's new command will be "right! over!" Click on the jump and treat.

Now, work on the left jump the same way you did the right. Point your target stick to the left jump and tell your dog "touch!" Click and treat. Then say "over!" Click and treat. Because your dog may naturally want to go to the right jump, don't click and treat if he does. Instead, hold the target stick out to the left jump and tell him to touch. Then, when he does, click and treat. Then say "over!" Click and treat.

Work with him on the left-hand side for a while, but don't let him forget the right-hand side. Continue to do a few right-hand jumps, but return back to working with the left side until you have him jumping consistently on the command "left! over!"

Once your dog is relatively confident in both left and right, it's time to put them together. Start with your dog between the two jumps, just far enough out so that he can choose between them and have enough room to jump. Tell him, "Shadow, left, over!" Use your target stick to direct him. When he jumps, click and treat. Now use the target stick to point to the right hurdle. "Shadow, right, over!" Click and treat. Vary which hurdles he needs to jump over. In other words, mix them up so he isn't always jumping one and then the other. If he still has problems with distinguishing, go back and work on the right and left sides individually before working again on adding the two together.

The last step is fading out the target stick. Fade it out by using your hand instead of the target stick.

## Definitions

**chain, chaining**—Putting two or more very distinct commands together to obtain a more complex action. An example of *chaining* is teaching a dog to go to a particular location, jump over a hurdle, and then sit. The dog must learn three separate behaviors that are not related. This differs from shaping in several ways, though it has a similar effect. Shaping is modifying a simple behavior to obtain a complex behavior. An example of *shaping* is teaching a dog to do a high five by touching a target stick.

## ★ Positive Method

Your dog should be loose for this exercise (in an enclosed area). Have a treat in your right hand. Put your dog in a sit and direct him over the right-hand jump with your right hand using the words "right! over!" Toss the treat over the jump. If he's used to following your hand, he'll go after the treat, and go over the jump. Give him praise. Practice this until he has an idea that he needs to go over the right jump to get his treat.

Now, work on the left jump the same way you did the right. Because your dog may naturally want to go to the right jump, use a treat in your left hand to lure him to the left jump. Then, when he does move to the left jump, toss the treat over and give him the command "over!" Praise him when he jumps over to get the treat.

Work with him on the left-hand side for a while, but don't let him forget the right-hand side. Continue to do a few right-hand jumps, but return to working with the left side until you have him jumping consistently on the command "left! over!"

Once your dog is relatively confident in both left and right, it's time to put them together. Start with your dog between the two jumps, just far enough out so that he can choose between them and have enough room to jump. Tell him, "Shadow, left, over!" Use your hand to direct him. When he jumps, praise him and give him a treat. Now, use your hand to point to the right hurdle. Give the command "Shadow, right, over!" Praise and give him a treat. Vary which hurdles he needs to jump over. In other words, mix them up so he isn't always jumping one and then the other. If he still has problems with distinguishing, go back and work on the right and left sides individually before working again on adding the two together.

# Summary

- Your dog doesn't need strict obedience training to learn how to play games in agility, but he does have to learn the rules of the game.

- Both you and your dog will have more fun on the obstacles if you learn the basics first.

- In order to eventually do obstacles, your dog needs to learn the following tricks using either the clicker method, a target stick, or other positive training techniques:

  Sit on command

  Lie down on command

  Come using the "here" command

  Go away from you using the "go out" command

  Jump over a hurdle

  Tell right from left

- Always keep training sessions from five to ten minutes a day.
- Always play after a training session.
- Keep your training sessions upbeat and end on a positive note.
- Have fun!

# 3

# Clicking with Agility (Obstacle Training)

Obstacle training is the first part of agility training. In obstacle train-ing, your dog learns how to jump over hurdles, climb over A-frames, and dash through tunnels. You and your dog will enjoy learning the obstacles together because it will challenge you both.

Obstacle training takes time. Start slowly and don't rush through the learning period. What appears easy for you is complex and new for your dog. A negative encounter with an obstacle may dampen your dog's enthusiasm for agility.

The best way to learn the obstacles is to take a course at a local training facility or club. Explain that you are training for fun, not competition, to make sure you find the class best-suited for you.

The A-frame, seesaw or teeter, and dog walk make up the con-tact obstacles. The dog must walk across them and touch contact zones to perform the obstacles correctly. Start with an easy obstacle such as the open tunnel or A-frame. Unless you've trained agility dogs before, it's best to leave the teeter, sway bridge, and closed tun-nel for later because they can scare a timid or nervous dog.

*Rush demonstrates great A-Frame technique.*

# A-Frame

The A-frame is a large contact obstacle that has two 8- to 9-foot ramps that meet at a peak in the center. The ramps are 3 to 4 feet wide. The dog must climb the A-frame to the top and then scramble down the other side.

## ✓ Clicker Method

Lower the A-frame if it's adjustable. This will make the A-frame less intimidating. At full height, it can frighten a dog. Clip a leash on your dog's flat collar and with a treat in one hand, lure him up the

## Good Starter Obstacles

- Open tunnel
- A-frame
- Hurdles
- Table
- Dog walk

## Contact Zones

On contact obstacles, there are certain zones, known as contact zones, that the dog must touch to successfully complete the obstacle. These zones are usually yellow. The dog must have at least one paw on the yellow zone to complete the obstacle. In competition, failing to touch the contact zone can disqualify your dog. But the underlying reason for contact zones is safety. If you allow your dog to leap off an obstacle without touching the contact zones, she could be seriously injured. Most handlers teach their dogs to pause on the contact zones.

A-frame and back down; click and treat. Do this very quickly so that your dog doesn't have time to be nervous or scared.

If your dog is nervous, keep his leash tight in one hand and a treat in the other. Try to keep him focused on the treat as you lead him across. Click and treat when you get him to the downside. After the next few times on the A-frame, your dog may climb it without encouragement. Click and treat each time when he's on the downside.

Now, it's time to put the cue word to the action. Use a command such as "frame" or "scramble" before your dog starts over the A-frame. Click and treat.

Once your dog learns to associate the command with the obstacle, teach him how to pause on the yellow contact zones using the command "wait" or "rest." To do this, slow your dog as he approaches the downward contact and command him to sit when he touches the contact portion.

Once your dog is comfortable with the lower height, raise the A-frame to the normal height. Practice at this new height several times to accustom your dog to it. When practicing at the full height, it's very important to keep your dog moving over the top to the downward side so he doesn't pause at the top and become fearful.

### ★ Positive Method

Lower the A-frame if it's adjustable. This will make it less intimidating. Use a command such as "frame" or "scramble" and lead your dog over the A-frame.

If your dog is nervous, keep his leash tight in one hand and a treat in the other. Try to keep him focused on the treat as you lead him across. Praise him and give him a treat when you get him to the downside. After the next few times on the A-frame, your dog may climb the A-frame without encouragement. Praise him and give him a treat each time he's on the downside.

After the next few times on the A-frame, your dog may climb it without encouragement. Teach him to pause on the yellow contact surface using the command "wait" or "rest." To do this, slow your dog as he approaches the downward contact and command him to sit when he touches the contact portion.

Once your dog is comfortable with the lower height, raise the A-frame to the normal height. Practice at this new height several times to accustom your dog to it. When practicing at the full height, it's very important to keep your dog moving over the top to the downward side so he doesn't pause at the top and become fearful.

# Dog Walk

The dog walk is a tall obstacle that has two narrow ramps joined by a long plank. The dog must walk up the ramp, while touching the contacts, cross the long plank, and then walk down the other ramp, touching the contacts. There are two sizes of dog walks: one with 8-foot-long planks and the other with 12-foot-long planks. The 12-foot dog walk is much taller than the 8-foot variety. The planks are 9 to 12 inches wide.

Lure your dog slowly across the board with a treat and click (or praise) and treat each few feet.

## Kiana's Favorites

Kiana's favorite obstacles were the A-frame and the tunnel. She liked A-frames because she could look out over the crowd. She loved scrambling up the A-frames because they are sturdy and didn't require her to worry much about footing.

She also loved tunnels. If there was a tunnel nearby, it immediately sucked her in (I call them "dog vacuums"). She had so much fun, it was hard to prevent her from performing tunnels when she saw them.

German Shepherd Dog, owned by Pamela Brown, learning the dog walk in agility class.

If you've prepared your dog for the dog walk with walking a plank, your dog shouldn't have too much trouble with walking across an 8-foot dog walk. (If you can find the smaller dog walk, it's less intimidating.) After your dog becomes comfortable with the shorter dog walk, you can advance to the 12-foot version.

## Preparing for the Dog Walk

You may be surprised that most dogs don't pay attention to where their back feet are. Most notice their front feet and their back feet just follow along. This works well except when a dog has to gauge where he needs to put his back feet, such as on the dog walk.

Start by laying a ladder on the ground and walk your dog through the rungs. He may find this scary or no big deal. Use a lure and click and treat as you lead him across.

Next, you'll want to train your dog to cross a smaller version of the dog walk. Purchase four cinder blocks and a board that is 12 inches wide, 8 feet long, and an inch or more thick. Lay the cinder blocks in equal distances on their sides and place the board flat on top of the cinder blocks so that they solidly support the board. Use a treat to lure your dog on top of the board, or if your dog is small, pick him up and set him on the board. Click and treat if your dog gets on the board or once the dog has all four paws on it.

**Kiana's Accident**

Kiana once took a tumble off the dog walk early in her training. After that, she was frightened of the dog walk and wouldn't go over it no matter how hard I tried to convince her it was safe. We took a break from agility for a while and when we came back to it, she had forgotten her fear of the dog walk.

Accidents can happen, so be very watchful when working with your dog. One mishap like Kiana's spill can sour a dog on a particular obstacle. You want this to be fun, not scary.

## ✓ Clicker Method

With a treat in hand, lead your dog up the ramp, focusing her attention on the treat rather than the obstacle. Keep her head lowered to force her to focus on the obstacle and not on the height. Click and treat as she walks onto the dog walk and once she has crossed the top plank and is on the downward side. It is very important to lead her quickly along; otherwise she may pause and become nervous about being so high off the ground. Click and treat at the end, before she steps off the dog walk.

Practice this a few times. If she is nervous, be sure to have her focus on the treat. Have a helper steady her on the opposite side of the dog walk. Once she is confidently performing the dog walk, add the cue word "walk" or another appropriate word. Teach her to pause at the contact patches using "wait" or "rest" as a cue word. Be sure to click and treat for stopping at the contact zones.

## ★ Positive Method

With a treat in hand, lead your dog up the ramp, focusing her attention on the treat rather than the obstacle. Keep her head lowered to force her to focus on the obstacle and not on the height. Use the command "walk" or some other appropriate word. It is very important to lead her quickly along; otherwise she may pause and become nervous about being so high off the ground. Lead her across the walk portion, then down the ramp, stopping at the contact patches with the command "rest" or "wait." Give her praise and treats. Practice this a few times. If she is nervous, be sure to have her focus on the treat. Have a  helper steady her on the opposite side of the dog walk.

### Backchaining

Some dogs, especially large ones, may find the dog walk intimidating. Another method of training the dog walk is called *backchaining*. In backchaining, the owner sets the dog on the downward ramp and walks the dog off. The owner then sets the dog a few feet farther up the ramp and walks the dog off. After the dog becomes comfortable with the new position, the owner moves the dog back a foot or so and begins the process again. In this way, the dog learns that in order to leave the obstacle, he must walk forward. You can also use backchaining for the A-frame and the seesaw.

Some people like to line the dog walk with small treats that the dog can pick up and quickly swallow. This focuses the dog's attention on the obstacle and not the height, which is very important with tall contact obstacles.

## Seesaw

The seesaw or teeter-totter is similar to the playground equipment, but without handles. The dog must enter the seesaw at the downward end, walk across it until he tips the plank, and then walk down the plank. This obstacle can be intimidating to new agility dogs

*Robyn, a Cocker-Golden mix, negotiates a seesaw.*

because it moves with the dog's weight. If the dog is unprepared for the seesaw to tip, it can crash down with a loud bang, scaring the dog. Like the A-frame and the dog walk, the seesaw has contact patches that the dog must touch on both the entry and the exit of the seesaw. Wait until your dog is comfortable with other obstacles before attempting the seesaw.

## ✓ Clicker Method

You will need a second person to help steady the seesaw while you lead your dog over it. Lead your dog onto the seesaw and click and treat. Now walk your dog slowly to just before the tipping point and click and treat. You and your helper should hold the other side of the teeter so your dog does not slam it down. As you move your dog forward, let the seesaw tip gently until the end touches the ground. Do not allow the seesaw to bang or it may spook your dog. Click and treat.

If your dog becomes fearful, stop everything and give him some time to calm down. Once he is calm again, click and treat. Don't allow him to rush off the teeter once he tips it. Instead, click and treat at the contact zone.

Once your dog is used to the action of the seesaw, you can start adding cue words. The first cue word is "seesaw" or "teeter," which will direct him to the obstacle. The next cue words, "tip it," let your dog know when he needs to tip the teeter. The final cue word is "touch," "rest," or "wait," for the contact zones. Always click and treat for these actions.

## ★ Positive Method

You will need a second person to help steady the seesaw while you lead your dog over it. Give your dog the command "teeter" or "seesaw" and lead him over the seesaw, using treats. Stop him just before

### Using a Helper

It helps to have a second person with you when you're teaching your dog the obstacles. He or she can help provide security along the other side of the dog walk while your dog is taking those first scary steps or hold your dog while you're at the other end of the tunnel calling her through it. Learning is much easier with a helper.

## Don't Force a Dog into a Scary Situation

I once saw a handler get bitten at a training class when he tried to push a strange dog onto a particular obstacle the dog was nervous about. When working with your dog (or with other people's dogs) be aware that if cornered and frightened, any dog may bite. This is why I always recommend positive reinforcing techniques rather than harsh techniques.

the tipping point and tell him "tip it." You and your helper should hold the other side of the teeter so your dog does not slam it down. As you move your dog forward, let the seesaw tip gently until the end touches the ground. Do not allow the seesaw to bang or it may spook your dog.

If your dog becomes fearful, stop everything and give him some time to calm down. Praise him and give him treats, and then start again. It may take a few times before your dog learns to tip the seesaw properly. Don't allow him to rush off the teeter once he tips it. Instead, put him in a sit on the contact area with a "wait" or "rest" command and then release him.

# Open Tunnel

The pipe tunnel or open tunnel is a favorite obstacle for most dogs. The tunnel is a large pipe with a 24-inch diameter that can flex into different shapes. The dog must enter the pipe tunnel, run through it, and then exit it.

## ✓ Clicker Method

Straighten the pipe tunnel and then push it together so that the tunnel is only a few feet long. Have a helper hold your dog and thread your dog's leash through the tunnel to the other side. Kneel at the other side of the tunnel while holding your dog's leash. Call your dog through the tunnel. You may need to lure him with treats and praise. Click and treat.

Practice the tunnel in this configuration a few times until your dog becomes used to it. Once he has learned the obstacle, use the cue word "tunnel" or another word to uniquely describe it and click

*Minnie, a Yorkshire Terrier owned by Debby Funk, makes it through the tunnel.*

and treat when he performs correctly. Then, lengthen the tunnel a bit and practice with the new configuration until your dog becomes comfortable with it. Continue to lengthen the tunnel in increments and train with the new length until it is at full length and your dog is confidently going through it.

At this point, add a small bend to the tunnel. Some dogs have no difficulty with not seeing the other side; others will refuse to go in. If your dog is nervous about entering what appears to be a closed tunnel, make the bend in the tunnel less severe so that he can see a little of the other side. As he becomes more confident with the tunnel, increase the bend. Eventually your dog should be able to enter a tunnel in a horseshoe configuration.

## ★ Positive Method

Straighten the pipe tunnel and then push it together so that the tunnel is only a few feet long. Have a helper hold your dog and thread your dog's leash through the tunnel to the other side. Kneel at the other side of the tunnel while holding your dog's leash. Call your dog through the tunnel. You may need to lure him with treats and praise.

Practice the tunnel in this configuration a few times until your dog becomes used to it. Use the command "tunnel" or another word to uniquely describe it. Then, lengthen the tunnel a bit and practice with the new configuration until your dog becomes comfortable with it. Continue to lengthen the tunnel in increments and train with the new length until it is at full length and your dog is confidently going through it.

At this point, add a small bend to the tunnel. Some dogs have no difficulty with not seeing the other side; others will refuse to go in. If your dog is nervous about entering what appears to be a closed tunnel, make the bend in the tunnel less severe so that he can see a little of the other side. As he becomes more confident with the tunnel, increase the bend. Eventually your dog should be able to enter a tunnel in a horseshoe configuration.

## Collapsed Tunnel

The closed tunnel, collapsed tunnel, or chute starts with a ridged circular opening. It then has a chute constructed from parachute material that the dog must push through to complete the obstacle. Many dogs new to agility find the chute daunting because it apparently goes nowhere. Dogs can accidentally become tangled in the chute,

*Dogs learn that the closed tunnel opens when you run through it, as Vapor, a Belgian Malinois owned by Lisa Dewey, demonstrates.*

## Preventing Accidents

The A-frame, the dog walk, and the seesaw can be hazardous because of the tendency for dogs to become nervous at their heights or movement. A nervous dog is likely to try to jump off these obstacles and can hurt herself. When training on these obstacles, you must redirect your dog's focus to the obstacle or to the treat or lure until she becomes confident with the obstacle. Always work with an assistant who can help balance your dog and make her feel more confident.

so it is very important to make certain it stays flat. Like the seesaw, this obstacle should be one of the last your dog learns. Your dog may find the closed tunnel disconcerting because he will have to push his way through the fabric.

## ✔ Clicker Method

Roll up the chute material and have someone hold your dog while you kneel at the other end. Hold the chute material open so that your dog can see you and the exit. Call your dog through. If your dog has learned the pipe tunnel, this new tunnel should not be of any concern. Click and treat when he enters the collapsed tunnel.

Once your dog is confident with the closed tunnel in this configuration, lengthen the chute material and allow a little sag in it. Call your dog. Your dog should walk straight through. Click and treat. Lower the chute a little at a time, allowing your dog to push through the material. Eventually you will be calling your dog through the closed tunnel in its final configuration.

Now add the cue word. Choose "chute" or something that uniquely identifies the collapsed tunnel. Some people use the same word, "tunnel," for both the pipe tunnel and the closed tunnel, only to regret it when they find a pipe tunnel and a closed tunnel side by side on a course!

## ★ Positive Method

Roll up the chute material and have someone hold your dog while you kneel at the other end. Hold the chute material open so that your dog can see you and the exit. Use the command "chute," or another unique word to identify the collapsed tunnel and call your dog through. If your dog has learned the pipe tunnel, this new tunnel should not be of any concern. Give him praise and treats. Try this a few times.

Once your dog is confident with the closed tunnel set up this way, lengthen the chute material and allow a little sag in it. Call your dog. Your dog should walk straight through. Lower the chute a little at a time, allowing your dog to push through the material. Eventually, you will be calling your dog through the closed tunnel in its final configuration.

# Hurdles

Hurdles or jumps are one of the most common obstacles your dog will encounter. They can be with or without "wings"—decorative panels on each side of the jump. Spread hurdles require the dog to jump two or three bars, and a broad jump requires the dog to clear several boards lying on the ground.

The height at which the jumps are set depends on the height of your dog at the shoulder. See chapter 2 for recommended jump heights.

If you have a puppy, you can still jump him provided that you keep the jump height low. Puppies should not jump hurdles higher than their hock height until they are full-grown. Ask your veterinarian when it is safe to jump your dog.

## ✓ Clicker Method

Start teaching your dog to jump by setting the hurdles at the lowest height. If your dog's maximum jump height is 8 to 12 inches, lay the

### See 'Em Wings?

Hurdles come in a variety of configurations. Some have wings or decorations along the sides that can be very distracting or even a bit scary. This is why it's very important for your dog to get exposure to as many types of equipment as possible.

As your dog has more exposure to unusual places and equipment, she'll become more confident.

*Sableman flies over a long jump.*

bar on the ground. Have your dog on a leash and lead him over the jump. Click and treat when he jumps it.

Next add a cue word, such as "over," "hup," or "jump."

As your dog becomes used to this height, increase the jump by one notch and practice at that height. If your dog is small, that jump may be at or close to his full jump height. If your dog is a large breed and you wish to jump over 20 inches, increase the jump height to 16 inches or so and practice there. Gradually move the bar up to full height. Your dog should learn what full height is like, but you should train at lower heights to avoid injuring your dog's legs. Use practice run-throughs at full height, but keep general practice jumps lower.

## ★ Positive Method

Start teaching your dog to jump by setting the hurdles at the lowest height. If your dog's maximum jump height is 8 to 12 inches, lay the bar on the ground. Have your dog on a leash and lead him over the jump. Give a command such as "over," "hup," or "jump." Offer treats to lure your dog over and give him treats and praise when he performs the jump.

As your dog becomes used to this height, increase the jump by one notch and practice at that height. If your dog is small, that jump may be at or close to his full jump height. If your dog is a large breed and you wish to jump over 20 inches, increase the jump height to 16 inches or so and practice there.

## Training Methods

Never use coercive or harsh training methods when teaching obstacles, and never force a dog to do something that is scary to him or will cause him to panic. You're likely to get bitten.

Gradually move the bar up to full height. Your dog should learn what full height is like, but you should train at lower heights to avoid injuring your dog's legs. Use practice run-throughs at full height, but keep general practice jumps lower.

# Tire

The tire jump is a hurdle with a tire or black irrigation hose in the form of a circle that the dog must jump through. It is the most technically demanding of the jumps because the dog often does not see it as a jump. Instead, the dog may try to walk underneath the tire. The tire's height is measured from the ground to the bottom of the inside opening of the tire. It is set at the same heights as other hurdles.

*Vapor, a Belgian Malinois owned by Lisa Dewey, tucks up through the tire jump.*

## ✔ Clicker Method

Train the tire jump as you would any other hurdle. Use treats to lure your dog through the jump and click and treat him when he complies. If your dog tries to climb underneath the tire, try putting a board or another jump in the open space below the tire. You may use the same cue word as for other hurdles or use a separate cue such as "tire" to differentiate it from other jumps.

## ★ Positive Method

Train the tire jump as you would any other hurdle. Use treats to lure your dog through the jump and praise him when he complies. If your dog tries to climb underneath the tire, try putting a board or another jump in the open space below the tire. You may use the same command as for other hurdles or use a separate command such as "tire" to differentiate it from other jumps.

# Table

The pause table is an obstacle that looks like a square table. It is set to the heights of the jumps. The dog must jump onto the table and perform a "sit" or "down" on command and remain there for a count of five.

Most dogs are used to jumping up on things (your dog may be allowed on furniture). In this case, the table is not a difficult obstacle. Teaching your dog to stay on the table for a count of five, however, may be more difficult.

## ✔ Clicker Method

Put the table in a short configuration, one that your dog doesn't have to work hard to jump up on. Lure your dog onto the table with a treat. Click and treat. Let her jump off again. Lure her back up. Click and treat. Now let her jump back off. Wait and see if she'll jump back on. If she does, click and treat. If not, continue to lure her and click and treat.

## Table of Many Colors?

In UKC agility, the dog is required to enter the side of the table corresponding with a particular color. While dogs don't see colors well, you most likely do and can lead him to the correct side and have him jump up on that side.

Once your dog is getting onto the table for a click and treat, add a cue word such as "table." Use the cue word before your dog jumps on it and then click and treat.

Now teach your dog to sit on the table. Give the command "table." After she is on the table, tell her to sit. Click and treat when she complies. Do this a few times until she gets the idea that she must sit on the table after she jumps on it. Once she understands that you want her to sit on the table, wait a second or two before clicking and treating. Slowly extend the time your dog waits until it is a full five seconds.

Next, teach your dog to lie down on the table. Lure your dog on the table and put her in a sit. Then tell her to lie down. (She may be confused, in which case use a lure or a target stick.) Click and treat. Once she understands that you want her to lie down on the table, wait a moment or two before clicking and treating. Slowly extend the time your dog will wait until it is a full five seconds.

You'll need to train both "sit" and "down" on the table until your dog is confident before increasing the height of the table.

## ★ Positive Method

Put the table in a short configuration, one that your dog doesn't have to work hard to jump up on. Lure your dog onto the table with a treat. Use the command "table" or another unique word for this obstacle. Use praise and treats to get your dog to stand on the table. Now, let her jump off again. Lure her back up and use the "table" command. Give her praise and treats when she climbs up on the table. Now, let her jump back off. Tell her "table" and see if she'll jump back on. If she does, praise her and give her treats. If not, continue to lure her up and give her plenty of praise and rewards.

*Golden Retriever Zippy, owned by Sue Johnson, waits on the pause table for the next command.*

Now, teach your dog to sit on the table. Give the command "table" and after she is on the table, tell her to sit. Give her praise and a treat when she complies. Do this a few times until she gets the idea that she must sit on the table after she jumps on it. Once she understands that you want her to sit on the table, wait a second or two before treating. Slowly extend the time your dog will wait until it is a full five seconds.

Next, teach your dog to lie down on the table. Lure your dog on the table and put her in a sit. Then tell her to lie down (she may be confused, in which case use a lure) and praise her and give her treats. Once she understands that you want her to lie down on the table, wait a moment or two before giving the treat. Slowly extend the time your dog will wait until it is a full five seconds.

You'll need to train both "sit" and "down" on the table until your dog is confident before increasing the height of the table.

## Weave Poles (Both Clicker and Positive Methods)

The weave poles are possibly the most difficult obstacle to master. They are PVC poles that are arranged in a straight line that your dog must weave through. Weaving is not intuitive to a dog so it must be learned.

A popular method of teaching weaves is the *channel method*. This requires either stick-in-the-ground weave poles or special training weave poles that will create a channel. The weave poles are arranged in two columns at the dog's shoulder width. Put your dog on a leash and have him run through the two columns for two weeks. (If you're using the clicker, click and treat after each run.) After that time, move the weave poles in 1 inch toward each other. When you run your dog through the columns, he will have to bend to move around them. Practice in that configuration for two more weeks. At the end of two weeks, move the poles in an inch and continue to practice with that for two more weeks. Eventually, the poles will move together to form a straight line and your dog will weave properly.

## Other Obstacles

There are other obstacles that are less common. These include:

- Crawl tunnel—a kind of tunnel the dog must crawl underneath.
- Cross-over—a towerlike structure that has four planks that meet in the center.

*Vapor demonstrates correct technique in the weave poles.*

- Hoop tunnel—a type of open tunnel the dog must go through.
- Pause box—a square made from PVC that lies on the ground. The dog must treat it like a pause table.
- Platform jump—the dog must climb on the box, sit, jump over the hurdle, and then sit again.
- Sway bridge—a small suspension bridge that moves as your dog walks over it.
- Swing plank—a plank that is suspended at the four corners. It moves when the dog crosses it.
- Tower—a structure that has a plank, stairs, and slide.
- Window jump—a jump shaped like an open window.
- Wishing well jump—a jump that looks like a wishing well.

# Summary

- Learning obstacles is a fun part of agility.
- Always teach obstacles using either positive reinforcement or clicker training. Never use coercive techniques.
- Use a helper when teaching obstacles. This will help your dog learn and provide a safe environment.
- Never force a dog to do something when he's fearful or panicking.
- The basic obstacles include:

  A-frame

  Dog walk

  Seesaw

  Open tunnel

  Closed tunnel

  Hurdles

  Tire jump

  Table

  Weave poles

- Some unusual obstacles you might see include:
    Crawl tunnel
    Cross-over
    Hoop tunnel
    Pause box
    Platform jump
    Sway bridge
    Swing plank
    Tower
    Window jump
    Wishing well jump

# 4
# Handling Your Dog

Now that your dog has learned the obstacles, you may think he's ready for agility. The truth is he only knows half of what he needs to know. Obstacles are only part of agility. The other part is called handling, and it's something that you must learn as well.

Agility is teamwork. It's not just performing obstacles. You must be able to direct your dog to the obstacle using both commands and nonverbal communication. If your dog is on a leash, this is easier, but eventually you'll want to train off-leash. By learning handling, you'll perform well as a team.

## On-Leash or Off-Leash?

In competition agility, you must run your dog off-leash. However, when you're just having fun with agility, you can run your dog on-leash, off-leash, or somewhere in between. The main concern is the *safety* of your dog.

If you can't trust your dog off-leash, you should keep him on-leash when training unless you train in an enclosed area. You don't want another dog to cross your path and possibly pick a fight. When training with a leash, be aware that the leash can snag on something and possibly choke your dog, so it is very important for you to have some way of cutting the leash, such as a pocketknife. This is also a good reason why you should never have a training collar on your dog when working in agility.

A compromise between a leash and no leash is a tab. A tab is sort of a mini-leash about 8 inches long with a knot on the end. You clip the tab to your dog's collar and use it to direct your dog where you need him to go.

Both the leash and the tab have their downsides, however. Both can get caught on equipment and possibly choke a dog. This is a trade-off if you're unable to control your dog off-leash. This is why it's important to carry a folding pocketknife or multitool that will enable you to cut your dog's leash if it gets caught.

## Your First True Sequence

At some point, you need to think about your dog performing more than one obstacle. After all, agility is more than just doing the A-frame or the tunnel. Putting a few obstacles together and running them together is called *sequencing*.

**Learning the Symbols**

Look at the various symbols for obstacles (see Figure 1). These symbols are fairly standardized for obstacles internationally. Course designers lay their courses on a 10-by-10 grid with each square being 10 feet square. You'll see particular course layouts that you can try with your dog. Some are intended to teach you and your dog new moves; others are actual courses you might see in competition. This book offers courses for learning new things plus having fun.

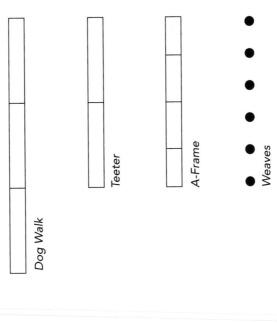

Fig. 1. Symbols for various obstacles.

Dog Walk

Teeter

A-Frame

Weaves

Hurdles

Tunnels

Closed
Tunnel or
Chute

Tire

Table

## Definitions

**entry point**—The place where your dog enters the obstacle.

**sequence**—A small portion of a course that the dog runs as a group.

**sequencing**—Putting two or more obstacles together and running them as a unit.

**trap**—Two obstacles, often side-by-side, where a dog can choose the incorrect obstacle.

You may have already inadvertently started sequence training. Maybe you've had several pieces set up and you've run your dog from the tunnel to the A-frame and over a jump. Congratulations! That's a sequence. Go ahead and set up a sequence now with some of your equipment. Use three pieces of equipment for the time being. Now run your dog from one obstacle to the next.

Is that all there is to sequencing? Yes and no. Certain types of sequences will make you into a better handler and challenge your dog. For example, a sequence that has a tricky entry point or a trap is more challenging than one that is in a straight line. I've included a few basic sequences to try (see Figures 2 and 3).

If you've done the exercises in chapter 2, your dog knows to watch your hands as well as listen for your commands. Start at your first obstacle and direct your dog to it with both a command and your hands. Remember to keep your hand flat and use your entire hand and even body to point toward the obstacle. When your dog completes the obstacle, click and treat (or praise and reward) him. Do the same for each subsequent obstacle.

## Handler's Tips

The great thing about agility is that you can use your whole body and not just your voice or hands to direct your dog to the obstacle. Your dog quickly becomes used to watching your entire body rather than just listening to your voice.

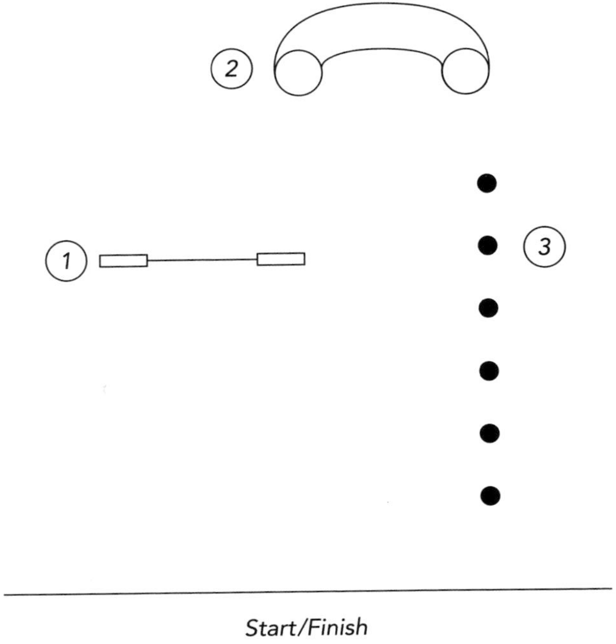

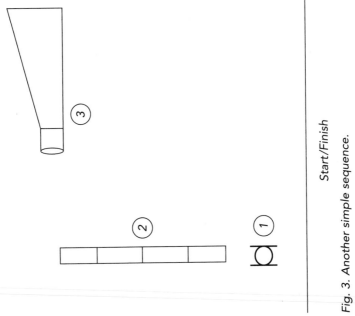

1
2
3
Start/Finish

Fig. 2. A simple sequence.

1
2
3
Start/Finish

Fig. 3. Another simple sequence.

## Communicating with Your Dog

You need to communicate to your dog which obstacle to take. Direct your dog to an obstacle by keeping your hand closest to the dog open and flat. Push your hand out toward the obstacle as though pushing it away. Say the name of the obstacle as you push toward it. At first, your dog may seem a little puzzled by this, but he will soon pick up your signals and come to expect them.

As you become more proficient with sequences, eventually you'll want to put those sequences together in a mini-course. But don't rush it; both you and your dog need to become comfortable with running the sequences before running a course.

# Handling from the Right Side

Handling from your dog's right side (your left side) may seem very natural if you've taken any obedience courses with your dog. Obedience training almost exclusively requires that the dog maintains heel position on your left side (his right side). You may notice that in agility, we're more concerned with your position *in relation to your dog,* not your dog's position in relation to you. So, when I talk about handling from the right side, I mean handling on your dog's right side.

Look at the sequence in Figure 4. This sequence is designed to keep your dog on your left-hand side or to handle him from the

## Why Handling on Different Sides Is Important

You may choose to have your dog run on either your right or left side in agility. Because there are no restrictions or limitations, sometimes handling from one side is better than handling from the other. Perhaps running your dog on a particular side just feels more natural. Often handling your dog on a certain side is the shortest way for you to travel around the obstacles.

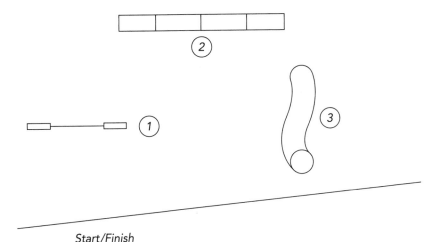

*Start/Finish*

*Fig. 4. Handling on the right.*

right. Your dog jumps the first hurdle, goes over the A-frame, and runs through the tunnel. When you follow along to direct him to the next obstacle, you'll be running alongside your dog on his right side (your left side). If you want to, you can try to run this on your dog's left side without crossing over and see what happens. It makes more sense to stay on the dog's right side instead of handling on his opposite side.

Can you choose to handle on the opposite side? Of course, you can! In some instances, maybe you want to. But your dog will be faster than you, so the less steps you have to take, the more likely you are to keep ahead of him.

## Handling from the Left Side

Now that you know how to handle from the right side, you need to learn how to handle from the left side. This will feel odd if you're used to doing obedience, but don't worry; it's easy to learn.

Look at the sequence in Figure 5. It may look familiar; it's the reverse of Figure 4 that you used to handle on the right side. By running this sequence in reverse, it gives you an idea how to look at a course and judge what makes the most sense for you and your dog.

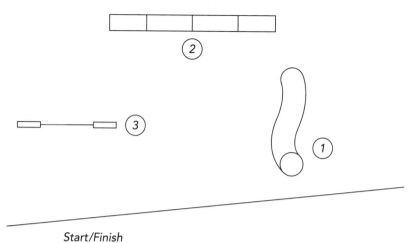

*Start/Finish*

*Fig. 5. Handling on the left.*

# Recalling Your Dog over Obstacles

Being able to recall your dog over obstacles is useful at the beginning of a course where there are a series of fast obstacles (jumps) followed by a slow obstacle (a contact obstacle or weave poles). This is especially useful if your dog is a very fast dog or if you have difficulty keeping up with him.

Start training your dog with one bar hurdle. Put your dog in a sit-stay in front of the bar hurdle with enough distance between your dog and the hurdle so he can clear it. (If your dog doesn't know "stay," see chapter 2.) Go around the hurdle and stand behind and to the side of it. Call your dog with a "here!" command. As he starts forward, tell him, "Shadow, over!" Praise and reward him or click and treat.

## Agility Tip

There is no one right way to handle a dog. Different breeds and temperaments will require various handling. Not all dogs will handle the same as a Border Collie. An Alaskan Malamute may require different handling than a Shetland Sheepdog; a Yorkshire Terrier will need different handling than a Golden Retriever. Don't believe someone when they tell you that you must only handle in one particular way. Every dog is different, and the fun of agility is learning what works for your dog.

## "Why Don't You Get a Real Agility Dog?"

I heard this often when I was trialing Kiana. Kiana was a difficult dog to handle due to her idiosyncrasies. She was stubborn, willful, and had a wicked sense of humor. What's more, she was fun to work with—if not frustrating. Very few people get to see Alaskan Malamutes work agility courses, whereas Border Collies and Australian Shepherds are common. Yes, some breeds are better at agility, and the statistics prove it. But that's not why I do agility. I do it to have fun with my dogs. I would rather work slowly with Kiana, who is dear to my heart, than trade her in for a Border Collie who could learn these things more easily.

If your dog becomes confused and goes around the obstacle, try clipping a long line or Flexi-lead to your dog's flat collar and stand in front of the bar hurdle holding the leash and allowing it to gently drape across the bar. Call your dog again and retract or reel in the line. As your dog approaches the jump, command him "over!" If he balks because the bar is too high, set it lower and try again. Once your dog goes over the bar hurdle, praise or click and treat him.

Once your dog learns that you want him to go over the bar hurdle when you call him, recalling him over two or more should not be difficult. Your dog must first become proficient with each hurdle before you add an additional one.

## Handling Nightmares

One thing to keep in mind is that not all handling will work for your dog. If you have a fast dog, doing a slow technique may make things difficult. Handle your dog the way you need to, not the way someone tells you.

Kiana was famous for not working the way trainers told me she ought to work. Once a trainer tried to get me to send Kiana over more than two hurdles away from me. Unfortunately, Kiana was very focused on staying beside me instead of going out. Kiana went over one and the second and turned right back to me. She seemed to think that two obstacles were her limit for working away from me.

This was maddening to the trainer, but I understood. Kiana was a sled dog who usually had responsibilities that would keep her close to me.

# Cross-in-Front

You will not always want to stay on the same side when handling your dog. After all, there are some sequences that need to be handled first from the left and then from the right. In this case, you'll want to learn how to either cross in front of or cross behind your dog. A cross-in-front, or cross-over, is where the handler crosses in front of the dog before the dog reaches a piece of equipment.

Typically, you do a cross-in-front when your dog is slow or is on a piece of equipment that slows him down (a table, contact obstacles, or weave poles). Look at Figure 6. You'll see two hurdles, a table, and a tunnel. Let's say you start by handling your dog on the left, which makes sense because of the two jumps. Now send him onto the table. While counting, you can cross in front of your dog to change sides to send him on to the tunnel.

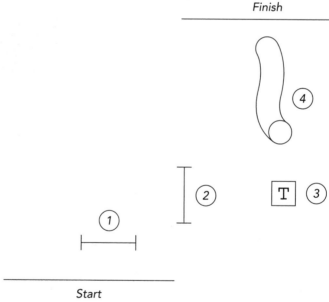

Fig. 6. Cross-in-front.

# Cross-Behinds

A cross-behind is where the handler crosses behind the dog, who is usually committed to a particular obstacle, or is done when the dog is so fast that the handler must change sides once behind the dog.

Let's look at the same sequence (Figure 7), only we'll run it in reverse for the cross-behind. Handle your dog on the left when you send him through the tunnel and direct him to the table. (Don't cross just yet!) Now send your dog over the hurdle and while he commits to the hurdle, cross behind and call him with a "here!" Now send him over the second hurdle.

That wasn't easy, was it? Practice sending your dog to commit to other obstacles and cross behind him. Slower obstacles such as contact obstacles, tables, and tunnels as well as hurdles can all be crossed behind the dog.

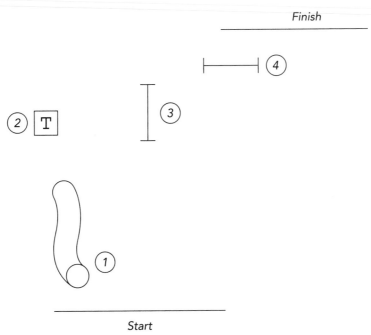

Fig. 7. Cross-behind.

Sableman, a Cocker Spaniel owned by Pam Metzger, taking the tire with ease.

Look, Ma—I can fly! Gideon the Brussels Griffon.

# Summary

- Obstacles are only part of agility. The other part is the teamwork between you and your dog.
- Learn to communicate with your dog, using commands and body language that enable you to direct your dog to various obstacles.
- Think safety first when handling your dog. It's ok to have your dog on a leash, but be sure to keep the leash from snagging on equipment.
- Sequences are groups of obstacles that are run together as a unit.
- You can run your dog on your right or left side.
- Following the shortest path is often the best way to negotiate an agility course. You can use the following techniques for the most fun and efficient run-throughs: recall your dog over obstacles, cross-in-fronts, and cross-behinds.
- Every dog is different. Handling has to be adapted to each one.

# Part Two

# Having Fun and Playing Games

# 5

# Fun Games and Courses

Now that you and your dog know obstacles and the basics of handling, you're ready to start putting together courses. This chapter shows how to create courses and set up some fun runs for both you and your friends. Some incorporate silly things dogs enjoy, such as food, toys, and other objects you would not see on a competition agility course.

## Choosing a Site for Your Agility Equipment

When you set up an agility course, it's best to look for level ground so that your equipment won't tilt. Since most agility equipment is heavy, it's nice to find a place where you can leave the equipment out and move it around only as you need it, like your backyard.

Remember that you don't need all the equipment. Hurdles, a tire jump, a table, weave poles, and tunnels are lightweight and inexpensive to make or purchase.

Choose an enclosed area for your training. Dogs can and do escape—even well-trained ones at agility and obedience trials. Because you'll be letting go of the leash on obstacles, such as the tunnel or the chute, it's very important to have a backup leash in case your dog *does* get loose.

# Designing a Course

If you feel ambitious and are looking for various agility courses, investigate the Internet resources at the back of this book. Be aware that many courses are aimed at those who are planning on competing, not just having fun.

When planning an agility course, look at what equipment you have and what your dog is capable of doing. Beginning dogs can seldom handle call-offs (an obstacle in the natural flow of the course that isn't the next obstacle to take), sharp turns, and traps well, so when you create a course, it should flow smoothly from one obstacle to the next with enough room for the dog to maneuver. You'll also want to plan on how to speed up or slow down your dog. Some obstacles are naturally accomplished quickly (hurdles and tunnels), while others tend to slow dogs down (contact obstacles, weave poles, and the table). You can choose how fast or how slow your course is by choosing the obstacles you put in it.

If the course is only for yourself and your own dog, then your only limit is your imagination, your equipment, and your dog's ability.

---

### Definitions

**jumpers**—A type of fast-paced course that uses only jumps and tunnels.

**jumpers with weaves**—A version of the jumpers course with weave poles added. This is primarily an AKC invention.

---

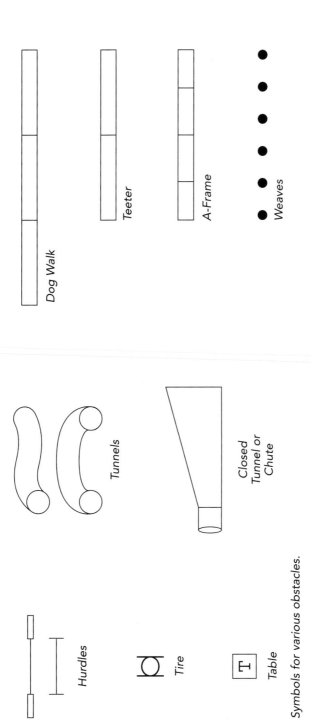

Dog Walk

Teeter

A-Frame

Weaves

Tunnels

Closed
Tunnel or
Chute

Hurdles

Tire

Table

Symbols for various obstacles.

## A Simple Jumpers Style Course

This simple course would be more correctly called a "sequence," that is, a small portion of what you might see on an actual agility course.

When you lay out a course, you can do it on paper so that you have an idea how it will look before you move the equipment around. This course consists of two hurdles, a tunnel, and a tire jump. Note that it can be run in either direction.

This sequence could appear in a jumpers course or a standard course, if you were to train for competition. Your dog will start by jumping over two hurdles, running through the tunnel, and then jumping through the tire jump. In the opposite direction, your dog would jump through the tire jump, run through the tunnel, and then jump over the two hurdles.

## A Simple Jumpers Course with Weaves

You can put this course together using minimal equipment in a small space. This portion of a jumpers course, similar to ones found in AKC's Jumpers with Weaves, includes weave poles. Note that you can run this course in either direction. Your dog starts with two jumps, goes through the tunnel, and then pops out and takes the weaves. When run backward, your dog will go through the weave poles, through the tunnel, and then over the two jumps.

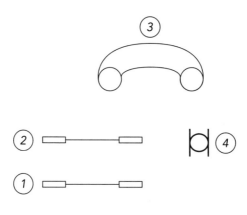

*Start/Finish*

*A simple jumpers sequence.*

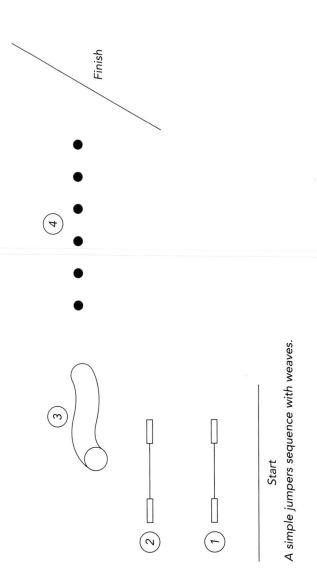

Finish

④

③

②

①

Start

A simple jumpers sequence with weaves.

## A Trickier Course

This is another simple course you can put together using a few pieces of equipment. I've added a contact obstacle in this, namely an A-frame, but you can use a dog walk instead. Your dog starts with two jumps and then goes to the A-frame, then into the tunnel and out.

This is a tricky course because dogs love the tunnel and it may take some handling to get your dog to take the A-frame instead. There are several ways to do this, but the best way is to handle your dog on your right side. As you run with him, you block his entrance to the tunnel and direct him to the A-frame. When coming around the A-frame's side, you send your dog into the tunnel and out.

You can run this course backward, but it's less tricky. You do so by running your dog through the tunnel, over the A-frame, and then over the hurdles.

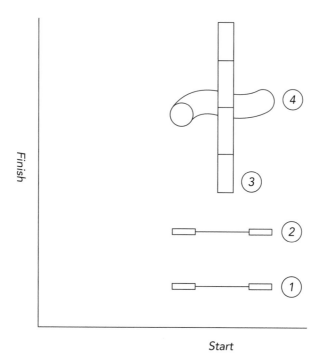

A tricky sequence with a trap.

## Experience at Matches

A few years back, Kiana and I attended a match with agility games that included a huge tunnel that first went up a ramp, then down a ramp, and underneath it. Kiana wasn't too sure about going upward in a tunnel, so we had to work on that a bit. But she got through it pretty well and by the end she was all smiles.

## A Standard Course in a Small Area

This gives you some ideas for how to create a "big" course in a tight area. Note that this is in a classic oval arrangement, which helps put the maximum amount of equipment in a tiny spot. (See the figure on the following page.) Start with the jump and proceed to the left teeter. From the teeter, have your dog take the tunnel, which puts him out toward the tire. Finally, have your dog go to the table and over the hurdle where you started.

You may notice that this course can be run forward or backward.

## An Eight-Obstacle Standard Course

This course lets your dog run nine obstacles in a very small space. (See the figure on page 91.) You can run this in either direction and have a lot of fun. First your dog goes over the hurdle and through the tire. Then he goes to the A-frame (or if you want a challenge, try the call-off and pull him to the tunnel). Next, he travels over the broad jump (or across the dog walk) and across the dog walk (or over the broad jump). From there, your dog goes through the tunnel (over the A-frame) and back to the tire jump. Once through the tire jump, he goes over the hurdle back at the start.

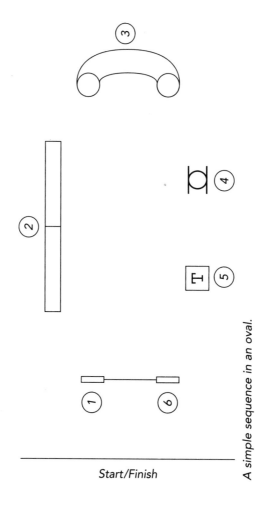

*A simple sequence in an oval.*

Start/Finish

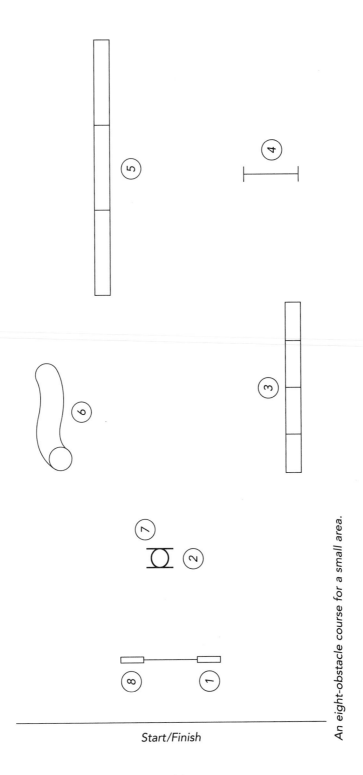

Start/Finish

An eight-obstacle course for a small area.

91

# Courses for Fun and Playing Games

Here are some fun courses you're not likely to see in any agility competition, using some nonstandard equipment. Try a few and see which appeals to you.

## Tons o' Tunnels (for One or More Teams)

If you were to take a poll on the most popular agility obstacle, you'd hear it was the tunnel, paws down! This course uses four tunnels, two contact obstacles, and two jumps for loads of fun. Start at the jump and go through the tunnel under the A-frame. Cross the teeter, go through a tunnel, and over the A-frame. Then go through a tunnel, over a hurdle, and through another tunnel. Finally, go over the teeter, through a tunnel, and back over the starting hurdle. Watch out, though; if you take the A-frame again, you'll be dizzy in no time!

## Weave o' Rama Race (for Two or More Teams)

This game requires more than one handler and dog team. Note that this requires two full sets of weave poles and six jumps. (See the figure on p. 94.) The object is to get through the course as fast and accurately as possible. You can run this as a single race or a relay if you have multiple dogs. The jump height needs to be set for the shortest dog (use the jump height guidelines in chapter 2).

Line up two courses side by side. Designate someone the judge to blow the whistle to start and also to let people know when a dog misses a weave poll. Call one team "red" and the other "blue." When the whistle blows, both teams start on the course, jumping over two hurdles and weaving through the weave poles. When the dog finishes the weaves, he jumps over the last hurdle, turns around and jumps over that hurdle again and back through the weaves. Once through the weaves, the dog must jump over the two hurdles to finish.

If, at any time, the dog knocks over a bar on the hurdle or misses a weave pole, he must start at the beginning of the course and do it all over again.

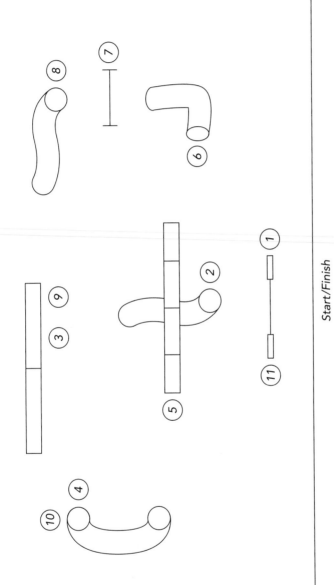

Start/Finish

Tons o' tunnels.

93

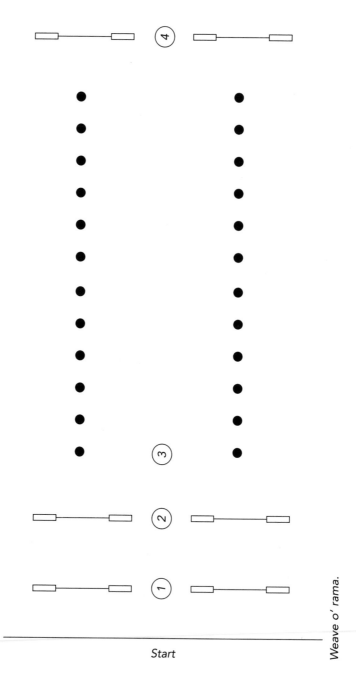

Finish

Start

*Weave o' rama.*

94

## Gambling Game (for One or More Teams)

If sequences aren't your thing, you'll enjoy the gambling game. (See the figure on the following page.) This game is based on Gamblers, which is available in two competitive agility organizations. However, unlike their version of Gamblers, this takes the gamble (a sequence) out of it.

In the gambling game, you can pick and choose what obstacles you'd like for points. You have thirty seconds to perform all the obstacles and tally up the points (the more points, the better).

The points go as follows:

Contact obstacles (including the table)—3 points

Tunnels, chutes, and the tire jump—2 points

All other hurdles—1 point

So, for example, your dog can take five jumps, the dog walk, two tunnels, and the A-frame for 15 points total. If you have more than one team, you can have races to see who gets the most points. It's helpful to have someone there as a timer who can also tally up your points, but it is not necessary. The great thing about the gambling game is that you don't need to have a set course.

## Splish-Splash (for One or More Teams)

If your dog is a water dog or if it's a particularly hot summer, you'll both enjoy splish-splash. (See the figure on page 97.) You'll need to purchase two baby wading pools and fill them with water for this game. Start with two hurdles and then go on to the A-frame. At the downside of the A-frame, you'll have one of the wading pools ready to go for a splash. Next will be another hurdle, followed by a tunnel and a hurdle. Right after the hurdle is another wading pool for a splash at the end.

## Hound (for Two or More Teams)

A fellow dog book author, Caroline Coile, recommended this game to me, adapted from her game Hound in her book *Beyond Fetch*. Have your agility equipment set up in a sequence or course. The first team starts with choosing an obstacle and performing it. Successful

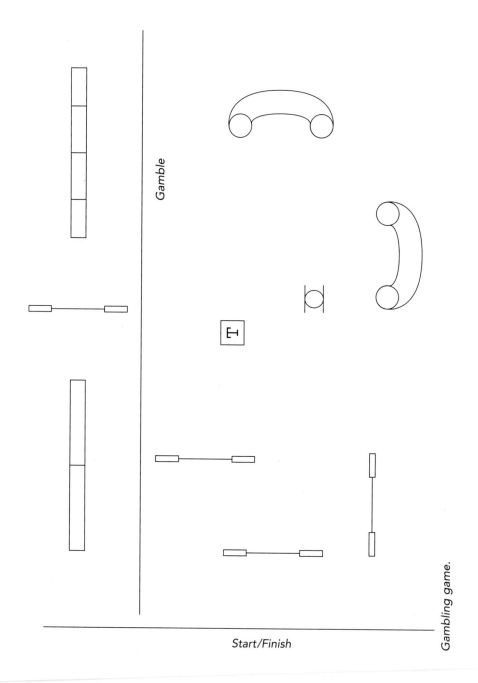

Gamble

Start/Finish

Gambling game.

96

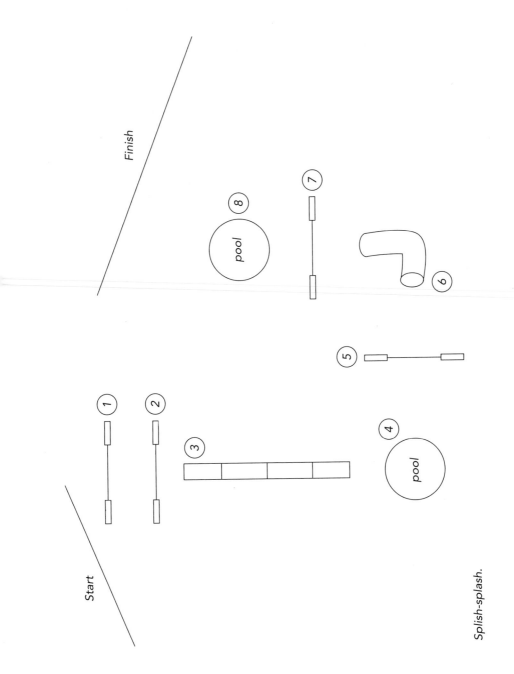

Start

Finish

pool

pool

*Splish-splash.*

completion of the obstacle earns the team an "H." The other teams then do the same obstacle for "H." Any teams that don't complete the obstacle are out.

Then, the second team chooses an "O" obstacle. The second team must do both the "H" and the "O" obstacle successfully. Each remaining team must then complete the "H" and "O" obstacle. Any teams that don't complete the obstacles are out. Then the next team chooses the "U" obstacle and has to perform the "H," "O," and "U" obstacles, and so on until there are no teams left or until the teams spell "HOUND." Those teams that spell "HOUND" are the winners.

## Agility Scavenger Hunt (for Two or More Teams)

Take some small plastic bags and put a small treat in each of them. Tie them with a ribbon and mark them from one to however many obstacles you have (make enough for each team at each obstacle). Place each bag with the number facing up next to the obstacle. (Hint: Mix them around.) Start a stopwatch to count down one minute. Now, have the first team start and look for the bags in sequential order. When they find the next bag, they must perform the obstacle to get the treat bag. The team stops when the time is called or they perform all the obstacles in order. The winner is the team with the most treat bags (dogs get the treats afterward).

# Flygility (for One or More Teams)

Flygility is a combination of the sport of flyball with agility. This is not a popular sport in the United States although there are clubs in New Zealand that promote flygility. However, it doesn't mean you can't have fun trying it.

Flygility is run like a relay race with a start and a finish line like agility. On the start, the dog runs through the agility course, hits the flyball box, grabs the ball, and finishes the agility course. Then, the next team goes forward.

## Flygility Equipment

Flygility requires a flyball box. A flyball box is a box with a hole and a lever. A tennis ball pops out of the hole when the dog steps on the lever. Plans are available in flyball books and on the Internet, or you may purchase a flyball box from an obedience supplier. You will also need tennis balls.

Flygility allows certain pieces of agility equipment, including hurdles, the A-frame, pipe tunnels, and weave poles. You can use flyball hurdles for this sport. Use them as the first hurdle from the start line and as the last hurdle before the flyball box.

## Training for Flygility

If your dog already knows agility, adding the flyball component isn't too difficult. First train your dog to catch tennis balls as you throw them up in the air. Then, change to the flyball box and teach your dog to trigger the mechanism. Some dogs become so proficient at knowing when the ball is ready to come out that they have their mouth open and waiting before it pops out!

It helps to have a dog that loves to chase tennis balls. If your dog knows how to play fetch, even better. Teach your dog to catch the ball when you throw it and then call him to you. Give the dog praise and treats when he catches it and brings it back. Use a command to catch the ball that you will use in flyball. Now, start throwing the ball in the same manner as a ball would come out of a flyball box.

Add the flyball box once your dog is proficient at catching the ball. Step on the flyball box and release a ball. Use a cue word associated with catching the ball in this new game. It may take a few times for your dog to catch the ball, but if he knows the command to catch, he will get the idea. Lavish praise and treats on your dog when he catches the ball from the flyball box.

Teaching your dog to trigger the flyball box is easy. Take your dog's feet and press them against the flyball box to release the ball. Give your dog the command to catch before the ball releases. If your dog is good, he may catch the ball as it shoots out. Even if he does not catch the ball, give him a treat and praise him for stepping on the box. Keep repeating the action until your dog gets the idea and starts catching the ball.

## The Flygility Course

You'll construct the flygility course just as you would an agility course but with a flyball box someplace in the middle of the course. In the flygility course I created, your dog will jump the hurdle, go over the A-frame, over another hurdle, and through the tunnel before reaching the flyball box. Once your dog triggers the flyball box, he goes through the six weave poles and over a hurdle to finish.

# Summary

- Having fun in agility doesn't always entail sticking to the rules.
- Try new courses and different combinations of equipment. Your imagination is your only limitation.
- Try new combinations of items to make agility more fun. Running weave races, adding pools of water, and even combining other sports with agility can add excitement.
- Invite your friends to try the new combinations. Maybe their creativity will help you come up with a new game or sport.

# 6

# Holding an Agility Party

What could be more fun than agility? Why, having an agility party, of course! Sharing agility with your friends and their canine companions is so much fun, you might want to consider having a party more than once a year—maybe to celebrate those special occasions like Christmas, Hanukkah, New Year's Day, St. Patrick's Day, Easter, Fourth of July, or Halloween. Or why not your dog's birthday or adoption day? Anytime is a good excuse for a party!

## Planning the Agility Party

Before you get on the phone and start calling your friends, make plans. Who are you going to invite? When will it be held? Can you hold it indoors if the weather is inclement? What about refreshments? How about invitations, prizes, and other things?

---

### Finding Local Agility Trial Schedules

You can find most of the agility trial schedules by checking them online at http://www.cleanrun.com/agilityinfo/events.

---

## When to Hold Your Agility Party

You can hold an agility party anytime, but you might want to hold your party on traditional holidays or on special dates. These dates might include:

- New Year's Eve/New Year's Day Celebration
- Valentine's Day
- Fat Tuesday (Mardi Gras, six weeks prior to Easter)
- St. Patrick's Day (March 17)
- Easter
- Cinco de Mayo (May 5)
- Spring equinox (April 21)
- Fourth of July
- Summer solstice (June 21)
- Halloween
- Thanksgiving
- Hanukkah
- Christmas
- Kwanzaa (December 26 to January 1)
- Winter solstice (December 21)
- Your dog's birthday or adoption day

Not only will you have a good excuse for a party, but you'll also have a good theme for it. Dogs can come in costumes for Halloween or receive presents from their secret Santas on Christmas.

Take your friends' schedules into consideration. Many people whose dogs know agility compete in agility as well. You don't want to throw a party and have nobody come because they're all at the big agility trial across town. The same is true for friends who show their dogs in obedience and conformation.

You can find out what is going on the weekend you're planning the party by asking a friend who is into competition. You can also go online and search for dog events in your area.

## What's the Theme?

Every party should have a theme. If your agility party is around a particular holiday, you can choose to adopt that theme. Fall, winter, spring, and summer are good themes for a party as well. Here are some ideas to get you started:

- Christmas—Santa Claus, snowmen, reindeer, holly, Christmas trees
- Fourth of July—American flags; red, white, and blue; the Statue of Liberty; Uncle Sam

*Cinnamon, a Golden Retriever, plays Santa Claus.*

*Easter bunnies Ginger, Cinnamon, and Audrey, ready to find their Easter eggs.*

- Cinco de Mayo—piñatas, Mexican flags, maracas, colorful Mexican blankets
- Halloween—costumes, ghosts, witches, werewolves
- Hawaiian—luaus, grass skirts, tropical drinks and foods, Hawaiian music, beach sand, shells, starfish
- Jungle safari—stuffed animals depicting wild animals, tropical plants, African art
- Victorian tea party—cups of tea, biscuits, crumpets, lace, flowers

Think about your interests and what you find fun and share that with your friends. The only limit to your themes is your imagination.

## Who Should You Invite?

Perhaps the question should be who *shouldn't* be invited to your party. When you choose participants, you'll want people whose dogs

## Printing Greeting Cards

You can make your own greeting cards using software such as Microsoft Publisher, PrintMaster, or Greeting Card Publisher. Most basic desktop publishing software will allow you to print color invitation cards without a lot of hassle. Or you can search the Web and find a greeting card site such as one provided by Hewlett-Packard at http://www.hp.com/go/ideahouse.

are relatively well-behaved. Avoid inviting friends with aggressive dogs and those whose dogs are completely out of control. You don't need a party to end up as an emergency trip to the veterinarian.

## Invitations

Your invitations should reflect your party theme. If you're a bit creative and own a computer, you can draw up an invitation on your computer and print it out. If you don't have a computer, you can purchase invitations at your local party or stationery store.

Regardless of whether you make or buy the cards, you should address the invitations to your friends' dogs from your dog. You might want to add a small biscuit or other treat before mailing it (be sure to add enough postage). You'll want to send the invitations with enough time for your friends to respond. Be certain to tell your guests to bring their humans, enough treats for training, clickers, and leashes. Also, ask the participants to bring their own water bowls and crates for their dogs.

## High-Tech Invitations

Who says you have to mail invitations? If all your friends are high-tech and have Internet access, you can e-mail your invitations. Some Internet Service Providers such as AOL allow you to "dress up" your e-mails with graphics and even sounds. This is a fun and paperless way to invite your friends to your party.

## Course Planning

As the big day approaches, you should decide on courses and games. Look through chapter 5 for possibilities. These might include:

- Tons o' tunnels
- Weave o' rama race
- Gambling game
- Splish-splash
- Hound
- Agility scavenger hunt

If you're planning on a full afternoon, you should probably choose two or three agility games. One or two games will keep your teams busy for two to three hours, depending on the size of the teams. Remember that it takes time to break down and set up new courses, so it helps if you have your first course set up before the guests arrive. Plan other games for the dogs as well.

## Games People (and Dogs) Play

You can intersperse the following games with your agility games:

- Bobbing for biscuits. Get a large shallow pan, such as a sheet cake pan and fill it with tepid water. Float several large biscuits in the water. Give each contestant a certain amount of time to grab all the biscuits he can. The winner is the dog with the most biscuits (or who has eaten the most biscuits).
- Treat hiding contest. This is great for parties in a park. Hide bags with dog treats along a particular path. The dog that finds the most bags wins.
- Distracted recalls. Have your contestants line up in sit-stays before a field of toys or treats with their owners on the opposite side of the field. Then, one by one, the owners call the dogs. The dog that comes to the owner without stopping for a treat or toy wins.
- Fish crackers. Test your dog's mouth-to-eye coordination. Have each contestant sit a certain distance away from his or her owner. The owner then tosses a fish cracker for the dog to catch. Each successful catch requires the owner to increase the distance by a few feet. The dog that can catch a fish cracker from the farthest distance wins.

*Zeus, a Smooth Brussels Griffon, asks
to be invited.*

- Pumpkin relay (great for Halloween). Buy some small, hollow foam pumpkins and plastic spoons. Have the owners balance the pumpkins on the spoons while holding their dogs' leashes. Split the owners into two or more groups. The owners and dogs must run to a marked line and back to their teammates while balancing the pumpkins. If they drop the pumpkin, they must start again. You can use small foam snowmen in winter or empty plastic Easter eggs in spring.

- Sock hop relay/ T-shirt relay. This is another dog-owner relay. The first dog starts out wearing either a human T-shirt or four human socks on his paws. He must run up and back with his human, keeping the clothing on him, or the owner must put it back on him. The next human-canine pair must take the clothing, put it on the dog, and continue the relay.

- Musical spots. Buy or pick up carpet sample swatches from a carpet store. Arrange them in a circle with one less than the number of participants. Have the owners walk the dogs in a larger circle or square around the swatches to music. When the music stops, each dog must sit on a carpet swatch. Any dog without a carpet swatch is out. Remove a carpet piece and repeat the game. The last dog left is the winner.

## Refreshments

What's a party without refreshments? Both owners and dogs will enjoy the party if you provide yummy treats for both species. Since there are plenty of recipe books for people parties, I'll let your imagination determine what you should provide for the humans.

Dogs, however, should have treats that they can enjoy. Remember that certain foods are poisonous to dogs and are strictly off limits. These include:

- Alcohol
- Caffeinated products
- Chocolate
- Grapes
- Onions

You can purchase treats (biscuits, soft dog snacks, and so forth) at a local pet supply store, but you can also make your own if you're feeling adventurous. If you purchase treats, be certain that they can be chewed and swallowed quickly because you don't want to have dogs fight over food.

## Agility Party Planning Timeline

One to two months ahead:

- Decide on a date for the party.
- Choose a place for your agility party and obtain permits (if required).
- Select an alternate place or date if weather is a factor.
- Ask for volunteers (course workers, judges, and so forth).

Three weeks ahead:

- Make and send out invitations.
- Purchase nonperishable party supplies.
- Plan party events, select games, and decide on refreshments.
- Pick out prizes.
- Purchase or make your dog's costume (if applicable).

## Useful Equipment for an Outdoor Party

- Awnings or umbrellas for shade
- Coolers for food
- A table
- Collapsible chairs
- Extra crates for dogs
- Water jugs

- Purchase gifts for volunteers.
- Purchase a few extra dog water bowls.
- Purchase or borrow an extra crate to keep on hand.

One week ahead:

- Make any dog treats.
- Put together any scavenger hunt bags.
- Check all equipment to be sure it's in good order.
- Send out any e-mail reminders to those who haven't responded.
- Coordinate with volunteers. Ask them to come an hour beforehand.
- Review the party schedule.
- Purchase several 2-gallon jugs of water for the dogs (if you don't have fresh water available).

Two days ahead:

- Purchase perishable food items and keep refrigerated.
- Prepare any dishes that can be made ahead of time and keep refrigerated.
- Purchase film for your camera or buy a disposable camera.
- Purchase any additional items needed.

One day ahead:

- Set up the first agility course.
- Double check all prizes, refreshments, equipment, and party plans.

## Apple Cinnamon Training Bits

4 cups whole wheat flour

1/2 cup cornmeal

2 tablespoons vegetable oil

1 teaspoon cinnamon

1 small apple, grated

1 1/3 cups water

In a bowl, combine the flour, cornmeal, vegetable oil, and cinnamon. Add the apple and water to the mixture. Mix until it starts clumping together. Turn out on a lightly floured surface. Knead well. Roll out 1/4- to 1/2-inch thick. Score (but don't completely cut through) the dough horizontally and vertically with a straight edge to make 3/4-inch squares. Place on a baking sheet that has been sprayed with a nonstick spray. Bake at 325°F for 1 hour. Break into pieces when cool. Yield: 1 1/2 pounds.

## Cheese Nuggets Dog Treats

1 1/2 cups hot water or meat juices

1 cup uncooked oatmeal

4 tablespoons margarine

1/2 cup powdered milk

1 cup grated cheddar cheese

1/4 teaspoon salt

1 egg, beaten

1 cup wheat germ

3 cups whole wheat flour

1 cup cornmeal

Pour the hot water over the oatmeal and margarine; let stand 5 minutes. Stir in the milk, cheese, salt, and egg. Add the wheat germ to the oatmeal mixture. Mix well. Add the flour 1/2 cup at a time. Knead 3 to 4 minutes. Add flour until the dough is stiff. Roll out the dough 1/2-inch thick and cut into shapes. Bake at 300°F on a greased cookie sheet for 1 hour. Turn off heat and leave in the oven for another 1 1/2 hours.

# Carob Treats

3 cups whole wheat flour

2 1/2 cups oatmeal

1/2 cup wheat germ

1/2 cup powdered milk

1 tablespoon brown sugar

2 ounces (about 1/4 cup) carob chips, melted

1 cup water

1/4 cup molasses

2 tablespoons peanut oil

2 tablespoons corn oil or margarine

Mix the flour, oatmeal, wheat germ, powdered milk, and brown sugar in a large bowl. Add the remaining ingredients and mix until blended. The dough will be stiff. Roll the dough 1/2-inch thick and cut into shapes. Place on a greased cookie sheet and bake at 300°F for 1 hour. Makes 2 to 3 dozen.

# Canine Cookie Bones

1 pound beef liver

2 cups water

1 1/2 cups toasted wheat germ

1 1/2 cups whole wheat flour

In a 2-quart pan bring the liver and water to boil over high heat. Cover and simmer over reduced heat until livers are no longer pink in the center, approximately 10 minutes. Pour through a strainer over a bowl, reserving 1 cup of the liquid. Cut the liver into 1-inch pieces.

Put the liver in a blender or food processor; whirl, add reserved liquid, and blend until smoothly puréed. Scrape into a bowl. Stir in wheat germ and flour until well moistened. Turn onto a lightly floured board; roll out dough to a 1/2-inch thickness. Cut with a bone-shaped cookie cutter. Place the bones 1 1/2 inches apart on a greased baking sheet. Bake in a 350°F oven until browned, about 20 minutes. Turn off heat and leave in the oven at least 3 hours.

Refrigerate in an airtight container up to 2 weeks; freeze for longer storage. Makes approximately 7 large, 11 medium, or 46 small bones.

# The Agility Party

The day of the party has arrived! You've double-checked your schedule, prepared your goodies and prizes, and set up your agility equipment. If you've planned your party carefully, everyone should have a great time, but here are some helpful tips to keep things running smoothly:

- All dogs should be on a leash to avoid squabbling or running off.
- Owners should have their crates and water bowls available.
- Costumes must be off when the dogs enter the agility course (to prevent getting the costumes caught).
- Watch for overheating.
- Designate one of the volunteers as the photographer.
- Use your volunteers to help move items, judge, time the dogs, and other things, but be sure that they have fun, too, and aren't stuck with doing chores all the time.

*Waiting for the party to begin.*

*Whippet and owner dress for a Fourth of July party.*

## Schedule

The schedule of events will help you keep everything running smoothly. It will also help prevent conflicts. For example, if you're planning on having dogs come in their costumes, you should plan on judging the costume party before any agility to prevent possible costume snags on the equipment. You should also intersperse nonagility with agility games to give you and your volunteers time to change the equipment.

It's probably better to plan too many games than not enough. You can always remove a game or two from the schedule if a particular event is going long.

## Judging

You'll need judges for your games as well as for your costume contest. When you have volunteers, give them set criteria for judging and let them make the call. After all, this is for fun, not serious competition.

## Sample Party Schedule

**Refreshments:**

Humans—soda pop (variety), cookies, potato chips

Canine—store-bought liver treats, Apple Cinnamon Training Bits, bowls of water

**Schedule of Activities:**

12:00 p.m.—volunteers arrive; brief them on courses and party

1:00 p.m.—guests arrive; dogs in costumes

1:30 p.m.—costume judging (remove costumes)

2:00 p.m.—agility scavenger hunt

3:00 p.m.—T-shirt relay

3:30 p.m.—fish crackers

4:00 p.m.—hound (agility)

5:00 p.m.—awards

In agility games such as the scavenger hunt and the gambling game, you'll need someone who will time the competing teams and tally each team's points. Judges are helpful in other games just to keep them fair.

## Prizes and Awards

Your prizes and awards can be as elaborate or as simple as you'd like. You can print out award certificates on your computer (Printmaster and Microsoft Publisher both have templates) or you can wrap a ribbon around a large dog biscuit. Other prizes might be tennis balls, stuffed dog toys, flying disks, rawhide chews, or other canine favorites.

At the end of the party, those teams that didn't win anything should receive some sort of consolation prize as a thank-you for attending. After all, you don't want them to feel left out, do you? Be sure to give your volunteers presents to thank them for their work.

# Summary

- Planning your agility party will make it go smoothly and successfully.
- Consider having a themed party. Possible themes may be seasons, holidays, or even a special date related to your dog.
- Make fun and unique invitations. You can e-mail invitations if all your participants have Internet access.
- Intermingle agility games with nonagility games for the most fun.
- You can purchase or make your own dog treats. Be sure you have plenty of refreshments for both dogs and humans.
- Make a detailed party schedule.
- Use volunteers to help judge, time the dogs, or move equipment around. Thank them with a present.
- Give out prizes for the winners, but don't forget to give everyone a prize at the end. This is for fun, remember?

# Part Three

# Health and Agility

# 7

# Emphasizing Good Health

Part of having a good agility dog is having a healthy dog. She can't have fun if she's hurt, sick, or injured. This chapter covers preventive care, vaccinations, lameness, and what to do if your dog gets injured.

## Vaccinations

Vaccinations are important to any dog, especially one who is active in a sport. Certain diseases, such as rabies and distemper, can affect any dog at any age. Your veterinarian can recommend an appropriate vaccination schedule.

### Vaccination Choices

Many vaccines are currently available. Unless your dog is at high risk for certain diseases, she probably does not need every one. You and your veterinarian should decide what vaccinations your dog needs based on his age and health, and the area of the country you live in.

*It's amazing how dogs learn to love the weave poles.*

Vaccinations also depend on the amount of exposure to other dogs. For example, if your dog uses the same agility equipment as other dogs, particularly those who frequent the competition circuit, your vet may want to add kennel cough to your dog's vaccination schedule.

Many veterinarians vaccinate once a year, but the current trend in veterinary medicine is to vaccinate every three years. In some cases, over-vaccinating has led to autoimmune disorders in dogs and cats. Talk to your veterinarian about a vaccination regimen that is right for your dog.

## Rabies

Rabies has been feared throughout the ages, and with good reason. Rabies is caused by a virus and is nearly always fatal. It is contagious to humans and is transmitted through the dog's saliva, usually through a bite. The incubation period varies anywhere from three weeks to three months or more.

Rabies takes two forms: dumb (paralytic) and furious. Both forms affect the central nervous system. In dumb rabies, the dog's throat becomes paralyzed, causing drooling and the inability to swallow. Furious rabies is the classic "mad dog" form, where the dog becomes vicious and attacks without provocation. Furious rabies eventually progresses to the paralytic stage, and death follows within a few days.

Most municipalities require dogs to have rabies vaccinations. The majority of vaccines are the three-year variety, meaning that the pharmaceutical company certifies that it is effective in dogs for up to three years.

## Canine Distemper

Distemper is highly contagious among dogs and may be transmitted through the air, on shoes, or on clothing. It is nearly always fatal. Distemper starts with a yellow-gray discharge from the nose and eyes, high fever, dry cough, and lethargy. It usually progresses to appetite loss, diarrhea, and vomiting. Distemper may affect the intestinal tract or may attack the nervous system, causing seizures and convulsions. Some dogs may have hardening of the pads, hence the name "hardpad disease."

## Canine Adenovirus 2

Canine adenovirus 2 is a form of highly contagious kennel cough. Dogs who contract kennel cough have a harsh, dry cough and may sound like they are gagging. Unless the dog is very old or very young, kennel cough is more of a nuisance than a danger.

*It's a bird! It's a plane! It's Sableman the Cocker Spaniel owned by Pam Metzger.*

## Infectious Canine Hepatitis

Infectious canine hepatitis is a form of adenovirus that causes fever, lethargy, jaundice, excessive thirst, vomiting, eye and nasal discharge, bloody diarrhea, hunched back, hemorrhage, and conjunctivitis. Infectious canine hepatitis may attack the kidneys, the liver, the eyes, and the lining of blood vessels. This disease may occur simultaneously with canine distemper. It's contagious to other dogs through an infected dog's urine, feces, or saliva.

## Canine Parainfluenza

Canine parainfluenza is another form of kennel cough. Dogs who contract kennel cough have a harsh, dry cough and may sound like they are gagging. Unless the dog is very old or young, parainfluenza is more of a nuisance than a danger.

## Leptospirosis

Leptospirosis is a bacterial infection that causes high fever, frequent urination, a brown substance on the tongue, lack of appetite, kidney failure, hunched back, bloody vomit and diarrhea, mild conjunctivitis, and depression. Dogs may contract leptospirosis from rats, infected water supplies, and infected dogs. It is contagious to humans. It can be fatal to dogs, and more deadly forms have also caused death in people.

## Canine Parvovirus

Canine parvovirus is a dangerous virus that causes severe, bloody diarrhea, vomiting, dehydration, high fever, and depression. Half of all puppies who contract it die. Canine parvovirus is highly infectious in dogs and is transmitted through fecal matter. The virus can live up to one year in the soil and can be carried on shoes or paws.

## Canine Coronavirus

Canine coronavirus looks a lot like a milder form of parvovirus and is transmitted through fecal material. Both parvovirus and coronavirus may infect a dog simultaneously.

## Bordetella Bronchiseptica

Bordetella bronchiseptica is a form of kennel cough. Dogs who contract kennel cough have a harsh, dry cough and may sound like they are gagging. Unless the dog is very old or very young, bordetella is more of a nuisance than a danger.

## Lyme Disease (Borellosis)

Lyme disease causes fever, lameness, loss of appetite, and fatigue in both animals and people who are bitten by infected deer ticks. Lyme disease is fairly common along the East Coast and upper Midwest in the United States, and continues to spread.

## Giardiasis

*Giardia* is a microscopic organism that lives in streams. Carried by beavers and other wildlife, as well as domesticated animals, Giardia was once confined to the Rocky Mountains, but may now be found in any untreated water. Giardia causes severe diarrhea, vomiting, and weight loss.

# Lameness: Preventing and Treating It

Chapter 1 discusses the importance of the health check as well as the importance of warming up your dog. No matter how careful you are, however, dogs in agility are athletes and may eventually strain something. But think of it this way: your dog could pull a muscle or injure his leg jumping off the couch, too.

The most common injuries are to a dog's front legs and shoulders. It may come as a surprise, but your dog bears around 65 percent of his weight on his front legs. This number increases substantially when he runs downhill or jumps.

Watch your dog when he jumps over an agility hurdle. He lands first on his front legs and then on his back legs. Your dog's carpals (wrist joints) and shoulders take quite a pounding each time he lands. If he lands wrong or if he overstresses the joints, tendons, and ligaments, he can injure himself.

## Preventing Lameness

The best way to treat lameness is to prevent it altogether. Injuries usually occur when your dog isn't properly warmed up and stretched or when he is tired and gets sloppy. Overenthusiasm or when your dog isn't paying attention to what he's doing can also cause injury, as can performing an obstacle incorrectly, such as leaping from contact obstacles. As your dog's handler, you need to be sure he navigates the equipment in a safe manner. When in doubt, slow down.

Always spend time to warm up your dog before beginning an exercise. Cold, stiff muscles tear easier than ones that have been warmed up. The colder it is, the longer you'll want to warm up your dog and keep him moving.

But injury can also occur when your dog isn't performing at his peak. Soreness can cause your dog to favor one leg over another. Anyone who has exercised knows how stiff and sore one's muscles can become, especially from overuse. Lactic acid, produced as a waste product, can make your dog's muscles sore indeed. You can reduce lactic acid buildup through a cool down period and also through proper hydration. Water helps flush the lactic acid from your dog's system.

## Hydration

Water is the most important nutrient for a dog. Even slight dehydration can greatly affect your dog's performance and can contribute to injury. Always have fresh water available. You can convince your dog to drink more water by adding something tasty to it (broth, dog food, or meat scraps). Of course, what goes in must come out, so you may have more potty breaks when you encourage your dog to drink.

## Massage

After your dog exercises, gently massage his legs, feet, and shoulders. If you're not sure how to massage your dog, ask a professional dog massage therapist (yes, they do exist!) or someone with experience. *Dog Massage* by MaryJean Ballner offers some nice, gentle massages that you can incorporate into your program. Start gently and use strokes that move toward the heart (to encourage circulation). If anything is painful to your dog, stop and have a veterinarian look at it.

One secret that sled dog drivers use is a liniment called Algyval. It's very difficult to find but works wonders. Some claim it's akin to snake

*Molly, an American Eskimo dog owned by Becky Thompson, has fun running the weave poles.*

oil, but I've used it on my dogs with success. (A word of warning—it's peanut-oil based, so don't use it if you're allergic to peanuts.) When I use it on my dogs, my own hands feel better, so there's something to it. It is very strong smelling, due to rosemary oil. It's very expensive, too: 4 ounces will cost you $30 or more, but it lasts a long time and you don't need to use much. Rub it into your dog's legs gently and it will ease the soreness.

## What to Do for an Injury

If your dog isn't putting any weight on a leg or there is severe redness, swelling, pain, or broken bones, seek immediate veterinary attention. If your dog becomes lame and it isn't too severe, you can try to treat it yourself. Most minor lameness can be treated with ice and rest with a little Algyval massaged in. Your dog will be your guide on this. While there are some dogs who are big babies and will yelp at the slightest touch, most dogs are fairly stoic and won't show pain until it becomes an issue. In other words, if your dog is favoring a leg, there's a good reason; it's not just to gain sympathy.

Diagnosing a limp can be a bit tricky. Slowly go through the stretching exercises mentioned in chapter 1. Be very careful because pain can cause even a docile dog to bite. If your dog strongly objects, he's really in pain and you'd better get him to a veterinarian for an examination. Feeling down the leg and flexing it in a normal motion

*Seeing spots. TJ the Dalmatian owned by Stephanie.*

will show you where it might hurt. Otherwise, it's a good bet it's the shoulder. (Pressing on the shoulder while holding the leg retracted might elicit a response—again, be very careful.)

When you find the injured spot, gently massage Algyval into it and ice it for a while. Note that I am *not* recommending medication. Medication does two things: it masks the pain and therefore masks the injury. While it may make your dog *feel* better, it's very hard to gauge when the injury has healed. Your dog may feel fine but that doesn't mean he's ready to do agility again. Frankly, if your dog is in pain to the point you think he needs medication, it's time for a trip to the veterinarian.

### Ice

Put ice on any of your dog's injuries, just as sports athletes do. In most cases a plastic resealable bag filled with ice laid across the affected limp is all that's required. If your dog has thin hair, you may want to wrap the ice bag in a towel to avoid damaging the skin. Check on the injury to be certain it doesn't get too cold. Usually icing the

**Good Medication Book**

One book worth having on your bookshelf is Deb Eldredge's *Pills for Pets*, published by Citadel Press, 2003. See the resources at the back of this book for information.

injury for an hour (20 minutes on; 10 minutes off) will help reduce swelling and inflammation.

### Medications

The problem with using medications is that quite often they can mask an injury and cause the dog to overexert himself and re-injure the limb. Only use medications on advice of your veterinarian.

Your veterinarian may prescribe aspirin or an NSAID (non-steroidal anti-inflammatory drug) such as Rimadyl, Metacam, Deramaxx, or Zubrin. These medications are not without controversy; some dogs have developed bleeding ulcers on NSAIDs, and Rimadyl sometimes causes or aggravates liver problems.

Other types of medication are steroids such as prednisone or prednisolone. These are good for short-term use and help in reducing pain and inflammation, but long-term use (over a period of several months) can have severe consequences, such as a suppressed immune system and other medical conditions. However, removing certain steroids abruptly can also cause severe health problems, so it is very important to follow your vet's advice when administering medications.

### Rest

Whenever your dog becomes injured, rest is mandatory. The amount of time depends on the injury and the prognosis.

**Dangerous Medication**

Some over-the-counter pain relievers are actually poisonous to dogs. Never give a dog acetaminophen (Tylenol) or ibuprofen (Motrin, Advil). While aspirin is relatively safe, you should administer it under your veterinarian's supervision.

*Flying high! Joyce Tessier's Gideon.*

*On to the next obstacle!*

## Alternative Medicine

Both chiropractic and acupuncture treatments are available for dogs. I've tried acupuncture on Kiana with little success, but others swear by it. Regardless of which treatment you decide to try, always choose a licensed veterinarian who is trained in these modalities. Otherwise, you run the risk of having your dog severely injured by someone who may not know what he is doing. The following organizations have a list of veterinarians skilled in these techniques:

- American Holistic Veterinary Medication Association— http://www.ahvma.org
- American Academy of Veterinary Acupuncture— http://www.aava.org
- American Veterinary Chiropractic Association— http://www.animalchiropractic.org

### What if the Injury Is Recurring?

If your dog is becoming chronically lame, it's time for a trip to the veterinarian. Your vet can determine if your dog is suffering from something more serious like a stress fracture, a torn ligament, or damaged tendons. He can also determine if there is another cause to your dog's lameness such as Lyme disease or arthritis. There are good treatments available for both of these conditions.

## Summary

- Be sure to have your veterinarian vaccinate your dog against dangerous diseases such as rabies, distemper, and parvovirus, especially if your dog is frequently exposed to other dogs.
- The best way to treat an injury is to prevent it in the first place.
- You can treat minor lameness due to sprains by icing the injury and giving rest. Use medications only under supervision of your vet.
- Serious and chronic injuries need veterinary attention.

# 8

# Nutrition for Your Agility Dog

Nutrition isn't something normally covered in an agility book. Yet dogs need a healthy diet to perform their best, as human athletes do. You wouldn't feel good if you ate just junk food. Skip the junk food and go with good nutrition. Some people will feed their dog whatever they can find on sale or buy the cheapest food in the largest bags. This is not always best for your canine friend. Your dog deserves a premium food formulated for optimal nutrition regardless of whether he's an athlete or just a house pet. This chapter covers the basics of performance dog nutrition.

## Feed Your Dog Right

Dog food isn't what it used to be. Premium dog food from even ten years ago can't compare nutritionally with what is available now. Many premium dog foods are more digestible, have better protein

*Hard work can make a dog thirsty.
Belgian Tervuren owned by Lisa
Kretner.*

and fat sources, and even have supplements such as omega-3 fatty acids, glucosamine, and probiotics. Dog owners largely have the sled dog and other canine athletes to thank for these nutritional advances. Veterinarians and canine nutritionists studied dogs in high-stress situations to formulate an ideal diet. The adult dog or maintenance versions are slightly different renditions of the performance kibble that working dogs eat.

Is there a difference between premium dog food and bargain brands? Yes! Premium brands often use higher quality ingredients that are more digestible than bargain brands. Although the bargain brands tout the same protein and fat levels, the meat and by-products in premium brands are better for your dog than the ingredients found in cheaper foods. If you compare the ingredients, you'll find less expensive brands filled with cheap sources of protein such as soy and bonemeal, as well as fillers, sugar, salt, and artificial colors and flavors. The amount of money you save by purchasing bargain brands is often offset by the amount of food necessary to obtain the same nutrition as a premium brand. If you must feed two to three times the amount of bargain dog food to obtain the same nutrition as a premium dog food it's not much of a bargain, is it?

When you choose a dog food, always purchase a recognizable premium brand that is easy to obtain. This is important when you discover you are out of dog food at 9 P.M. Worse yet, you don't want to search all over town if the pet boutique next door stops carrying your brand. It used to be that you had to purchase premium foods from pet supply stores and veterinarians. Now, some grocery chains carry premium dog foods. When in doubt, contact the dog food manufacturer and ask about digestibility percentages for the particular dog food you are considering. The higher the number, the more digestible the dog food is and the less you will have to pick up in dog feces. Some super-premium brands have over 85 percent digestibility.

Unless you're really working your dog hard in agility to the point where he is losing weight, he will need about 26 percent protein and 15 percent fat-by-weight dog food. A percentage or two on either side is all right. If he is working hard and dropping weight, consider a 30 percent protein and 20 percent fat-by-weight diet.

The brand of food you choose should state that it meets the nutritional guidelines set forth by the AAFCO (Association of American Feed Control Officials). Most major dog food companies comply with AAFCO regulations, but you should check regardless of the brand or manufacturer.

Choose a dog food with a meat source such as chicken or other poultry, beef, lamb, turkey, or by-products. By-products, depending on the ingredients, can actually be a better source of nutrition than meat. We don't like to think of our civilized canines chowing down on lungs, liver, heart, intestines, and other organ meats, but that is precisely what wolves, their ancestors, do. When a wolf kills an animal, it doesn't just dine on the muscle meat, it also eats the organs, smaller bones, hair, feathers, and fur.

## Look for the AAFCO Statement

When choosing a dog food, make sure it's nutritionally complete and balanced. The way to do that is to look for the AAFCO (American Association of Feed Control Officials) nutritional adequacy statement listed on the label. If one isn't there, the dog food can't be considered a complete and balanced food.

*A healthy dog is airborne.*

## Dry, Canned, Frozen, or Semisoft?

Pound for pound, dry dog food or kibble is the most economical. You are also more likely to have choices such as performance or maintenance, whereas other types of dog food may only have puppy and adult versions. Dry dog food is convenient, has a fairly long shelf life (six months to a year) and provides the most nutrition for the money. One negative to dry dog food is that it is less palatable than other types of dog food.

Canned dog food is usually very tasty, but is more expensive than equally nutritious dry dog food. You are often paying for water and extra processing. It has a good shelf life, but once you open the can, it can quickly turn rancid. Many owners like to mix canned dog food with dry dog food to increase the dry food's appeal.

### Water: A Very Important Nutrient

A dehydrated dog is not healthy. Be sure to provide plenty of cool, clean water from a known good source year-round. Dehydration can seriously affect your dog's health and performance.

Frozen dog food is relatively new. It is the most expensive type of dog food since you pay for freezing and storage. You are also paying for the water and processing. It is extremely savory, but can very quickly go rancid. Another type of food on the market is dog food rolls in the shape of logs. These are very toothsome, but they are expensive compared to dry dog food. You must refrigerate them once you open them.

Semisoft foods such as those in the shape of burger patties are often laden with artificial colors, fillers, preservatives, sugar, and salt. They are extremely desirable to dogs and have a good shelf life, but you must feed your dog large amounts to obtain adequate nutrition. Since there are no premium semisoft dog foods available, you may wish to avoid feeding them to your dog except maybe as a treat. There is a compressed dog food roll that is somewhat similar to semisoft dog food. It is usually very delicious and made with good ingredients, but it's expensive to feed to larger dogs. Once you open the roll, you must refrigerate it.

# Homemade Diets

It's quite the fad to feed dogs a raw diet along with raw bones. People will tell you that these diets cure a number of ailments including allergies, cancer, and other problems. They will also tell you that commercial dog food is the equivalent of junk food.

What's really going on here? Should you throw out that bag of kibble for chicken wings and celery?

Dog food has made significant advances in nutrition in the past twenty years due to intensive research. The culmination of that research appears in a bag of premium pet food. Unless you are a canine nutritionist or have done extensive research into canine nutrition, it is highly unlikely that anything you could put together would be balanced or provide all the necessary nutrients for your dog. Dog food undergoes extensive testing to be certain of the quality and the nutritional content of the food.

If you do decide to cook your own dog food, consult with a veterinarian who has experience in developing homemade diets. You should ask a veterinary school for a feed analysis to determine protein, fat, carbohydrate content, vitamins, and minerals. Certain

*A German Shepherd trains on the A-Frame.*

minerals, such as calcium, have specific ratios with other minerals. Too little calcium (as seen in an all-meat diet) measured against phosphorus can lead to hairline fractures and severe bone loss. Too much calcium can inhibit absorption of other essential vitamins and minerals.

## Nutritional Requirements of a Performance Dog

Most performance dogs benefit from a high-protein and high-fat diet such as the amounts in a premium performance dog food. Performance dogs require higher protein and fat levels than pets. The dog's body uses protein for building muscle and repairing injuries. Dogs on a low-protein diet are more apt to become injured than those on a high-protein dog food. Performance dogs use fat as an energy source more efficiently than carbohydrates. A high-fat/low-carbohydrate diet helps dogs work at their peak efficiency. The best fats come from animal sources.

You may wish to look for a pet food that contains omega-3 fatty acids. Omega-3 fatty acids are relatively new but have received a lot of press recently. Research suggests that these fats help reduce inflammation, lower blood pressure, and may even shrink certain types of tumors. However, too much is a bad thing, so don't supplement, except under the advice of a vet. Feed a dog food that is balanced and you shouldn't run into problems.

Research suggests that it takes at least six weeks or longer before you will see any effect due to a diet change. So, if you're constantly switching foods, you won't see a benefit or detriment from one particular food unless it's fed consistently.

## How to Feed Your Dog

Most dog food manufacturers give guidelines for feeding. Although they tend to be a bit heavy-handed in amounts, the purpose is to ensure that a dog is getting enough nutrition. Start with the recommended amount and split it up into two or three meals a day (feeding once a day can cause problems such as bloat, which is a life-threatening condition). If your dog is gaining weight on the amount you're feeding him, cut back a little at a time until your dog maintains her proper weight.

## To Free Feed or Not to Free Feed?

Free feeding is where you leave a bowl of kibble out all day long for your dog. Your dog can eat when he wants. It's convenient for you because you don't have to establish a feeding time. Free feeding seems ideal, but it is actually a bad idea. Many dogs are gluttons and will eat until they get sick or bloat. Those dogs that do not stuff themselves will overeat constantly. When you establish a feeding time, you determine when and how much your dog will eat. This should be a part of his daily training. Have your dog sit while you fix his meal. He will recognize you as his food provider rather than thinking the food magically appears in his bowl every morning.

### Food Allergies

Some dogs are allergic to certain ingredients in dog food such as wheat, corn, soy, or certain types of protein. With the popularity of lamb and rice diets, dogs are eating more lamb and many have developed allergies to it. If you suspect that your dog is allergic to his food, have your veterinarian test him for food allergies. If he is allergic to beef or chicken, your veterinarian may suggest a dog food with a novel protein source such as venison, fish, or kangaroo.

## Vegetarian Diets

Vegetarian diets are usually not suitable for canine athletes. Many dogs require higher protein from a good meat source and some are allergic to soy, which is the primary protein source for vegetarian diets. Dogs are carnivores and process meat more efficiently than humans. If you work your dog, be certain to feed him a good meat-based diet. Vegetarian diets cannot meet the protein requirements of a performance dog.

A benefit to establishing a feeding time is that you will notice when he misses a meal. When a dog that is normally a good eater misses a meal he may be sick.

# Table Scraps and Snacks

Because you're training your dog in agility, he's getting treats often. You should probably refrain from feeding him table scraps and other snacks during the day. Most owners overstuff their dogs with treats so when it comes time to train, they have to give "the good stuff" or the dog isn't very interested.

Table scraps are usually high in fat, salt, and carbohydrates. They're not very healthful for your dog and can cause an imbalance in his diet. Limiting his treats (including during training) to no more than 10 percent of his diet will ensure that he keeps a healthy and balanced diet.

# Agility Treats

What works as healthy agility treats? You can try the following and mix them up if your dog becomes bored with one:

- Tiny diced bits of lean lunchmeat or hot dogs.
- Tiny diced bits of cheese.
- Commercial training treats for puppies or clicker training.
- Homemade baked treats (listed in chapter 6) formed into bite-sized pieces.

*A German Shepherd trains on the teeter.*

- Diced liver (dried liver is better and less messy).
- Diced bits of carrots or celery. Do not use onions, garlic, raisins, or chocolate chips. These are poisonous to dogs.
- Popcorn (popped, without salt).
- Diced bits of compressed dog food rolls.

Note that none of these should be given in large quantities. You can probably come up with other ideas for agility treats for your dog. If he has a favorite snack or biscuit, break it up into training-sized pieces and use that.

## Summary

- Good health requires good nutrition. Feed an active adult dog food formula to an adult agility dog. Only switch to a performance blend if your dog is losing weight due to activity.
- Choose a brand of dog food that is complete and balanced according to AAFCO guidelines.
- Dog food comes in dry, canned, frozen, and semisoft forms. All have their advantages and disadvantages.

- It's difficult to formulate a balanced diet when developing your own dog food. Consult a veterinary nutritionist to help you balance your dog's diet properly if you go that route.

- Follow the dog food manufacturer's feeding recommendations and adjust accordingly.

- Don't free feed.

- You can come up with plenty of fun agility treats for your dog. Just be sure that snacks and treats make up no more than 10 percent of your dog's diet.

# 9

# Having Fun with Special-Needs Dogs

In previous chapters, I've talked about training and conditioning healthy dogs between the ages of one and eight years. But what about other dogs? Perhaps you have a young puppy, an older dog, or one who has a disability of sorts; can you still have fun with agility? After all, a puppy has a lot of energy, the older dog isn't exactly ready for retirement, and a dog who has a disability still needs exercise. Many agility organizations won't allow disabled dogs or dogs younger than one year to compete.

But you're not looking to do competition. You're looking to have fun, right? Can you still have fun with agility? For these dogs, the answer is a qualified yes. In this chapter, we will look at the special-needs dog and the way to modify training so you and your dog can have a safe and fun time.

# Evaluating Your Dog

You need to be honest with yourself when it comes to your dog. While I encourage people with oldsters to get their dogs off the couch for a healthy and long life, there is a point where your dog just can't do things a fit, active dog can do. Whether it's arthritis, an injury, or some other health concern, some dogs aren't able to do any type of agility and you shouldn't expect it from them. If you think your dog is borderline, sometimes a trip to the vet is worthwhile. Talking with your vet about your dog's health and whether your vet thinks your dog would be able to do a few simple obstacles might be a good idea. Some things, like mild arthritis, can be mitigated with aspirin or other NSAIDS (such as Rimadyl, Zubrin, or Dermamax) and nutraceuticals such as Glucosamine, MSM, and Chondrotin. Your vet can usually give you an unbiased opinion on your dog's health and may be able to make recommendations.

After your vet gives the okay, you can start planning how you're going to train your special-needs dog. Remember, your first concern should be for the safety, comfort, and health of your dog. Agility can be strenuous exercise. Your dog will need to rely on his senses, coordination, and balance. A dog who can't see can take a tumble off equipment; a puppy who may have no coordination may do the same. Normal agility equipment may be just too dangerous.

Both older and younger dogs have similar concerns when it comes to agility: joints. An older dog often suffers from arthritis, which can cause pain. Jumping and climbing may put undue stress on already painful joints. Puppies are growing and their growth plates (those bulges that make the puppy's forelegs look big) aren't fully attached to the bone yet. Repeated stress can cause injury and can cause the puppy to grow abnormally. Usually those growth plates close up sometime between one and two years (you'll need your vet to make a proper determination), and before that time, you shouldn't risk overstressing your puppy.

As I've said in previous chapters, puppies younger than six months shouldn't be doing agility with regular agility equipment. It can put a lot of stress on your puppy's joints. If you're planning on doing some type of agility with a puppy younger than six months, don't jump him and only do work that won't stress his body—such as walking him across a ladder or a plank, using the tippy board, walking through an open tunnel, or getting him used to having a towel draped over him and playing an agility version of peek-a-boo.

---

### Peek-a-Boo Agility Style

One way to get a puppy ready for the closed tunnel is to play a game called "Puppy in a Blanket." Get a treat and a towel or small blanket. Coax your puppy to find the treat under the towel by nosing under it and give him the reward. Increase the distance your puppy must slide under the towel when he's successful. (Never let him get tangled up or frightened under the towel.) Pretty soon, he'll be diving under the towel for the treat.

---

With a special-needs dog, you can do agility, but you're going to have to modify the obstacles and your expectations. Later I will discuss potential changes to agility equipment and what you can do to have a safe and fun time.

## Modified Agility Equipment

So, what kind of agility equipment should you use? If you're dealing with a dog who is either very young, very old, or has a disability, you'll need to modify some of the more challenging equipment so that your dog won't risk injury.

Let's look at the types of equipment you can substitute:

- **The ladder.** Laying a ladder on the ground makes for a good trainer or a substitute for the dog walk. Your dog will have to negotiate walking through the slats.
- **The plank.** Use three cinder blocks laid horizontally on the ground and put a plank 8 inches by 2 inches by 12 feet across them as a substitute for the dog walk.
- **Lowered A-frame.** Put the A-frame in its lowered position so that the highest portion is no more than two feet off the ground.
- **Tippy board.** Cut a flat piece of plywood about two feet by three feet and cut in half lengthwise a piece of round PVC pipe with a two-inch diameter. Lay the PVC pipe so that the cut side faces downward and lay the board across the pipe. You can use this to substitute for the seesaw.
- **Hurdles.** Lower to hock height and substitute it for standard jump heights.

- **Cardboard box and towel.** Cut both the bottom and top of a box open and lay a towel over the open ends. You can substitute it for a closed tunnel.
- **Wide weaves.** Use stick-in-the-ground type of weave poles in a wide pattern to train your puppy.
- **Straight tunnel.** Keep tunnels straight and without bends.

# Puppy Agility

You've just gotten a puppy or perhaps you've had a puppy a while and you're amazed by his seemingly boundless energy. But before you buy that A-frame, triple jump, or any other piece of agility equipment, remember that puppies are babies and have no sense when it comes to what is too stressful or difficult for them. Also, very young puppies have the attention span of a gnat, so you must be extremely patient with them. One moment, your puppy might be scrambling down a lowered A-frame; the next moment, he's chasing butterflies in the field.

## Puppy Training Rules

When dealing with puppies, keep these points in mind:

- Keep sessions ultra-short. No more than ten minutes training before play and no more than thirty minutes total each day.
- Provide a positive, fun experience for your puppy. Don't use anything scary.
- Don't overwork your puppy. Yes, he's a powerhouse, but he needs rest, too.
- No jumping younger than six months. No rigorous jumping between six months and a year. Keep all jumps below hock level.
- Train with lowered A-frame, ladder (and eventually the plank), and tippy board to prevent stress on joints.
- Use the cardboard box and towel to begin training for the chute.
- Keep the table at the lowest height.
- Take time to play. Your puppy needs playtime.
- Be patient. Don't rush your puppy.
- End training on a positive note.

## Puppy Training

Puppies need more than just basic obedience and agility training. Your puppy also needs socialization. That means he needs to experience various people and things in a controlled setting. Trips in the car to fun places, visits with friends who own friendly pets, and walks along busy streets should all be part of your puppy's education. The more things your puppy can experience positively, the more he is likely to enjoy agility and less apt to have problems with aggression or even phobias.

## Beginning Agility Training

Before you begin agility training, teach your puppy the commands in chapter 2, using some form of positive reinforcement such as clicker training. Be patient; at this age he won't be 100 percent reliable. When you feel he has a grasp on most of the commands, you can start with an obstacle or two.

First try something easy, like the tunnel, and maybe something a little scary, like a tippy board or the ladder. Work the tunnel as you would in chapter 3. With the tippy board or ladder, try walking your puppy onto it using treats as a lure. Walk the puppy across the ladder quickly or, if you're using the tippy board, let your puppy move across it and tip it quickly. He may be a bit fearful at first, but let him investigate the board and let him see that it's no big deal. (Sometimes steadying the tippy board with your foot helps, too.)

After your puppy has mastered one obstacle, move onto another obstacle, but go back to the obstacles he learned previously to both reward him for working so hard on a new obstacle and also to maintain his training on the old obstacles.

When your puppy has mastered the "baby" obstacles, you may be tempted to move on to the more serious obstacles like the teeter, a higher A-frame, or the dog walk. Wait until he's six months or older when he's a little more put together and a little less floppy and clumsy. He's unlikely to forget one spill or bad incident. He's also more likely to do stupid puppy things and may get injured. So watch and wait.

The main thing to remember when training a puppy under one year is that he is just a baby and won't be perfect. Even if you discover that your puppy is an agility protégé, it's better to keep it simple until he has matured a bit. Many owners go too fast too soon and burn out their puppies before they even grow up. Don't make that mistake. You have years of having fun with agility ahead of you; you don't need to push hard.

## Creating a Puppy Agility Course

When your puppy has learned enough obstacles, you may want to put together a puppy agility course. Good for you! Start by putting together some of the puppy obstacles, such as the tippy board and cardboard box and towel with lowered jumps, a tunnel, and the table. When you design a course, make it simple and in a flowing line without hard turns or call-offs. Also keep the course somewhere between three and seven obstacles.

In most circumstances, you'll still want your puppy on a leash because he's not reliable. Just remember to not allow the leash to snag on anything.

# Older Dog Agility

Opposite of the puppy is the older dog (one older than eight years). He's seen quite a bit and may be a bit arthritic, but he's got a few good years left in him. Like the puppy, however, he needs some help when it comes to agility. Don't expect him to jump normal heights. You should probably take the normal height mentioned in the previous chapters and reduce it by four to eight inches just to be on the safe side. If you're really not sure of his joints, dropping the height to hock height (like a puppy) is safest.

As with a puppy, you're going to want to work with the simple obstacles first. This means working with the ladder and then the plank before attempting the dog walk. Work on a lowered A-frame

### Fitness and the Older Dog

Your older dog will be healthier and more active if he is fit. Excess weight can age your dog quickly and put stress on his joints and bones. Keep your older dog lean and fit.

before raising it. Try using a tippy board before going forward with the teeter. Start with jumps at hock height and slowly increase until they're at the full height. All these are good tips to keep your older dog safe.

## Agility and the Disabled Dog

If you own a disabled dog, you may be wondering if you can do agility with him. The answer depends a lot on the dog's disability and health. Some disabilities such as deafness can be worked around. A deaf dog doesn't need to hear to do agility; he needs to understand hand signals and must learn to watch you.

With a dog who is blind or has severely impaired vision, the problem is tricky. Your dog can't judge jumps and therefore is more likely to blunder into them rather than jump over them. Standard dog walks, A-frames, and seesaws are definitely out because they're too dangerous and your dog could become injured if he were to fall off. But that doesn't mean he can't learn puppy obstacles. Straight tunnels, tippy boards, ladders (and eventually the plank), and wide weaves are all good obstacle choices for the blind dog. You'll have to take this much slower than if you had a sighted dog, and you'll be guiding him through the obstacles both with touch and with your voice. You'll be his seeing-eye human! Never put him in a situation where he'll feel trapped or fearful, because he's relying on you to make this a fun and safe experience.

Lastly, the other potentially disabled dog is one who has lost a leg due to injury or cancer. Again, you're going to have to keep agility simple. That means jumps at hock height, straight tunnels, wide weaves, and no regular contact obstacles (use the ladder and tippy board only).

In most circumstances when dealing with disabled dogs, you're not looking to compete, but rather to provide some challenge and stimuli for your dog. Remember that you must be very patient with these dogs and stay close to provide support and safety in this activity. With the possible exception of a deaf dog, you should never allow a disabled dog to work with these obstacles at a distance; keeping near the dog may help you prevent him from injuring himself.

# Summary

- Puppies younger than six months should not do standard agility.
- Have a veterinarian evaluate your special-needs dog before trying agility.
- You can substitute easier obstacles such as the tippy board, the ladder, the plank, the wide weaves, and the straight tunnel for harder obstacles.
- Keep jump heights below hock level in most circumstances.

# Part Four

# What's Ahead—
# Getting Involved

# 10

# Where to Go from Here

Agility is a lot of fun, no doubt about it. Perhaps at some point, your dog will be doing so well that you'd like to do more. Perhaps you've been watching other handlers who have earned titles on their dogs and thought to yourself that your dog is at least as good as theirs—maybe better. Maybe you'd like a little to show for all the training you and your dog have put in. Many handlers who now compete originally started out training for fun. But when they saw how much their dogs enjoyed it, they kept going.

There are those of us who should belong to AA (Agility Anonymous) if there was one. Although there are no twelve-step programs for agility addicts, there are several clubs promoting agility. Within these clubs, you can be as competitive or as relaxed as you want to be.

*Sableman, a Cocker Spaniel owned by Pam Metzger, sailing over the high jump.*

# Just for Fun Agility

The trainer Bud Houston decided that agility was getting so competitive that people were losing sight of the original purpose of agility, which was to have fun with their dogs. So Bud created an organization known as JFF or Just for Fun.

It costs nothing to join; there are no special fees or memberships, and no cost to sanction events. The handler chooses the desired jump height for his dog, so if his dog is older and he doesn't want to stress her joints, there is no problem.

## JFF Contacts

Just for Fun (JFF)
8738 Slocum Road
Ostrander, OH 43061

Phone: (740) 666-2018
E-mail: dogwoodbud1@earthlink.net
Web site: http://www.dogwoodagility.com/JustForFun.html

## Definitions

**match**—A competition where no titles or competitive points are given out.

**trial**—A competition where a dog may earn points and titles.

## JFF League Play

One of the big draws to JFF agility is its league play. Each team consists of five dogs and handlers who play against eight other teams in the league in a weekly competition for eight matches. The top four scores earn the team a placement.

What makes this so fun is that you get to compete with your teammates for the best team in your league. Someone is always rooting for you and your dog to do well. However, if you don't do well, your score may be the one that gets dropped.

## JFF Matches

Holding a JFF match is free; however, you must send information to the JFF headquarters regarding the match so that if there are any qualifiers, JFF can cross-check them.

JFF allows the agility competitors to compete in beginning, intermediate, and advanced categories all at the same time. Titling fees are just $10 per title and the handler must keep track of his or her own score on a dance card.

## My Own Start in Agility

When I started training with Kiana, my white Alaskan Malamute, agility was still very new where I lived. There were no competitions at which to earn titles. But after a while, agility became popular and competitive, and Kiana earned dual titles in AKC and UKC trials. She retired at age eight due to wrist problems and lived happily until she was eleven, when she was diagnosed with bone cancer.

Agility is still fun and competition hasn't dampened my enthusiasm for the sport. My newest agility dog, Haegl, loves it as much as Kiana did, so while we train for fun, it's likely that one day we'll get around to competition.

## JFF Titles

**Beginner Agile Dog (BAD)**—three qualifying scores from the Beginner, Intermediate, or Superior classes.

**Mulligan Beginner Agile Dog title (MBAD)**—one or more of three qualifying scores were earned from a second-chance round.

**Intermediate Agile Dog (IAD)**—five qualifying scores from the Intermediate or Superior classes.

**Mulligan Intermediate Agile Dog title (MIAD)**—one or more of five qualifying scores were earned from a second-chance round.

**Superior Agile Dog (SAD)**—seven qualifying scores from the Superior class.

**Mulligan Superior Agile Dog title (MSAD)**—one or more of seven qualifying scores were earned from a second-chance round.

**Games I**—four qualifying scores from at least two different games played at the Beginner or Advanced level.

**Games II**—seven qualifying scores from at least three different games played at the Beginner or Advanced level.

**Games III**—ten qualifying scores from at least four different games played at the Advanced level.

# Competitive Agility

I brushed on competitive agility in the previous section by talking about competing in league play and obtaining titles, but I haven't really talked about competition. I competed in agility for a time with what would be considered a noncompetitive dog: an Alaskan Malamute.

Competition can be daunting. If you have the wrong mindset and are concerned with only high scores, titles, and placements, you can quickly make yourself and your dog totally miserable in competition. Some dogs don't have the ability to handle the stress or achieve high scores. People who dwell on performance can easily become angry at their dog for missing a contact or taking a wrong course. Those with performance anxiety find themselves wrapped into a ball of nerves every time they step into the ring.

## Definitions

**refusal**—When a dog passes by, turns away from, or refuses to perform a particular obstacle.

**off-course**—When a dog performs the wrong obstacle or an obstacle out of sequence.

**fly-off**—When a dog leaps off the teeter as it tips and doesn't touch the appropriate contact patch.

**missed contact**—When a dog performs the obstacle but doesn't touch the required contact patch.

**four-paw rule**—If a dog places all of four paws on a contact obstacle, but fails to complete the obstacle, the dog isn't allowed to take that obstacle again.

**NQ**—A nonqualifying run.

---

Competition isn't cheap, either. Trial entry fees can cost $15 to $50 per day, depending on how many run-throughs and how many classes you're competing in. (Some, like USDAA and NADAC, have three or more classes.) It costs more if you're running a second dog, not to mention other expenses (travel, food, and in some cases, lodging).

Those are the negatives of competition. There are plenty of positives, however. You can demonstrate to your friends and your peers what a wonderful dog you have and what a good handler you are. You can earn titles on your dog—even if he's not a purebred or has never been registered with the American Kennel Club. It's also fun to show up on the agility course with an unusual breed. People perk up when they see a dog other than a Border Collie, a Golden Retriever, a Shetland, a Sheepdog, or an Australian Shepherd. (Many people tried to guess what breed Kiana was because she was an unusual all-white dog.)

One advantage of competition is that you start meeting new friends and seeing old ones. Soon people will be cheering for you and your dog because they know who you are. Almost everyone wants your dog to qualify. It's also amazing to see people drive in from other states to compete in your local trials.

Most important, competing *is* fun. There's nothing like preparing to go to a trial and setting up your blanket, your dog's crate, your picnic lunch and cooler, and everything that you and your dog need to spend the day. You talk with friends and watch other people compete. Maybe around noon, you take a break and walk your dog to the nearest fast-food restaurant for a hamburger (and don't forget one for your dog). Then you compete and get to show off your dog. All that can be fun.

## Agility Organizations

There are many national agility organizations currently available. Each organization has its own flavor of agility. Most are variations of on another, but there are some substantial differences in timing and handling.

When I wrote my first agility book, *Introduction to Dog Agility*, there were four major national organizations: the American Kennel Club (AKC), the North American Dog Agility Council (NADAC), the United Kennel Club (UKC), and the United States Dog Agility Association (USDAA). Since that time, the Australian Shepherd Club of America (ASCA) and Canine Performance Events (CPE) have joined the ranks. The good news is that you can compete and earn titles in all but AKC if you have a mixed breed, and if you have a purebred (even if unregistered) you can compete in all forms of agility.

*Gideon loves the weave poles so much, he barks all the way through. Brussels Griffon owned by Joyce Tessier.*

---

## Rules in Competitive Agility

Competitive agility differs from just-for-fun agility because of the rules. For example:

- In AKC Standard agility classes, dogs can be penalized for refusals.
- Dogs can NQ ( not qualify) for taking a wrong course.
- Dogs can NQ for violating the four-paw rule and for fly-offs.

There are other rules regarding competitive agility, most dependent on the various organizations.

---

That leaves you with quite a choice, doesn't it? You may be wondering which form of agility is right for you and your dog. If you have the chance to try out all forms, by all means, do so. Some, like USDAA and NADAC can be pretty fast-paced. Others, like UKC, focus more on handling and less on your dog's time (though timing is important). Some, like UKC, also have special times to take into account people with disabilities. You may not be able to place in the top scores, but your dog will be able to qualify and earn titles.

A few organizations have two divisions with two sets of jump heights and times. These divisions were developed to allow more dogs to compete for titles who would normally not be able to successfully compete in the more competitive classes.

A number of organizations also have junior and veteran divisions. In the junior divisions, the handler is younger than eighteen and receives special titles for qualifying in that division. In the veteran classes, the dog is older than a specified age and is allowed to perform at lower jump heights and usually slower speeds.

These recent developments have made agility competition open to virtually every healthy dog. Agility has spread throughout the United States and throughout the world. With so many agility organizations and clubs internationally, you will probably find one or more style available to you. If you're very lucky, you may have four or more styles to choose from. See the resources at the back of this book for a full listing of agility organizations.

## American Kennel Club (AKC) Agility

AKC offers a variety of titles in both Standard and Jumpers with Weaves. They allow only purebred dogs either with regular registration or ILP (indefinite listing privilege) registration. ILP dogs must be neutered.

AKC offers two levels of events: regular and preferred. The regular classes have jump heights at 8, 12, 16, 20, and 24 inches. The preferred classes jump heights are at 4, 8, 12, 16, and 20 inches with an extra five seconds added to the regular classes.

## Australian Shepherd Club of America (ASCA) Agility

Despite its name, ASCA allows other breeds and mixed breeds to enter its agility trials. It follows the rules put forth in NADAC agility trials and often trials with ASCA and NADAC are dual sanctioned. ASCA requires handlers who wish to obtain ASCA titles for their dogs to register with ASCA as well.

## Canine Performance Events (CPE) Agility

CPE offers five levels of competition. They have both Standard and Games classes and allow both purebreds and mixed breeds to complete. CPE offers a junior handler program and a veterans program, with extra time added for those with disabilities.

In order to obtain an agility title with CPE, your dog must show proficiency both in Standard and Games classes. The courses are as follows:

- Standard course—obstacles including contact obstacles, weave poles, hurdles, and tunnels.
- Jumpers course—hurdles and tunnels.
- Colors course—the handler chooses from one of three mini-courses and runs it successfully.
- Wildcard course—the handler chooses between wildcard obstacles set side by side. For each wildcard obstacle completed, the handler gets a certain amount of points. The dog must complete enough wildcards to qualify.
- Jackpot course—the handler chooses the obstacles the dog performs to earn points until the whistles blows. The dog must then perform the "gamble" before the time runs out. The gamble is a prechosen sequence of obstacles at a required distance from the handler (like Gamblers in NADAC and USDAA).

- Snooker course—the dog must perform the obstacles (set up in a "standard" or "modified" snooker configuration) according to a particular color pattern. The opening snooker sequence begins where the handler must direct her dog through the obstacles in a "red-color-red-color-red-color" pattern where the "color" is any color object the handler chooses. Each color object has a different point value. Once the dog completes the opening sequence, he finishes with the closing sequence of "yellow-green-brown-blue-pink-black."
- Fullhouse course—the dog must accumulate enough points (similar to playing poker) to obtain a three of a kind (three hurdles), two of a kind (two open or closed tunnels, or a tire jump), a joker (one contact obstacle, a weave, or a double or triple hurdle), the pause table, and enough points to qualify.

## North American Dog Agility Council (NADAC) Agility

NADAC offers a fast version of agility based on British rules and allows purebred or mixed breed dogs. An overwhelming number of different titles are available in all varieties (Standard, Gamblers, Jumpers, Tunnelers, Weavers, and Touch 'n Go) of classes in Novice, Open, and Elite. They also present junior handler's and veteran's classes and provide a jump height exemption list.

One of the fun things about NADAC is not only the huge number of titles your dog can earn but also the variety of courses available. The courses include:

- Standard course (Regular Agility Class)—obstacles including contact obstacles, weave poles, hurdles, and tunnels.
- Gamblers course—the handler chooses the obstacles the dog performs to earn points until the whistles blows; then the dog must perform the "gamble" before the time runs out. The gamble is a prechosen sequence of obstacles at a required distance from the handler.
- Jumpers course—hurdles and tunnels.
- Tunnelers course— tunnels exclusively.
- Weavers course—tunnels and weave poles.
- Touch'n Go course—contact obstacles and tunnels.

## Teacup Dogs Agility Association (TDAA)

TDAA is open to any dog, regardless of breed or mixed breed, who is 17 inches or less at shoulder height. Smaller dogs may compete in either Standard or Games classes (similar to the approved games in JFF). Jump heights are set at 4, 8, 12, and 16 inches. Long-backed, veterans, and deep-chested dogs all jump one height lower than the normal height.

## United Kennel Club (UKC) Agility

This version of agility is based on control and preciseness. UKC offers Agility I, Agility II, and Agility III courses. UKC equipment varies considerably from AKC, NADAC, and USDAA in their Agility II division. All dogs are allowed to compete with UKC registration, provided mixed breeds are neutered.

One interesting thing about UKC's agility is the unusual set of obstacles one might see on the Agility II and the Agility III courses. Agility I has fairly standard equipment: hurdles, teeter, A-frame, dog walk, table, and open and closed tunnels. Agility II has unusual equipment such as crawl tunnels, sway bridges, swing planks, pause boxes, and platform jumps. Agility III has a mixture of both types of equipment.

UKC allows handlers with disabilities to run their dogs at the speed at which the handler can move. This is very important for those handlers who have mobility problems or who are confined to a wheelchair.

## United States Dog Agility Association (USDAA) Agility

This is a faster version of agility based on British rules. USDAA offers standard, jumpers, relay, snooker, and gamblers courses. USDAA offers a Championship program and a slower performance program as well as a junior handler class. All dogs, purebred or mixed breed, are allowed.

A positive development in USDAA agility has been their adoption of the performance program. Jump heights in the performance program are 8, 12, 16, and 22 inches compared to the much more difficult jump heights of the championship program which are 12, 16, 22, and 26 inches. The A-frame height has been lowered to a maximum of 5 feet, 6 inches (from 6 feet, 3 inches), there are no spread hurdles, and each course time has three more seconds added to it.

The courses you'll see in USDAA agility trials include:

- Standard course (Regular Agility Class)—obstacles including contact obstacles, weave poles, hurdles, and tunnels.
- Gamblers course—the handler chooses the obstacles the dog performs to earn points until the whistles blows; then the dog must perform the "gamble" before the time runs out. The gamble is a prechosen sequence of obstacles at a required distance from the handler.
- Jumpers course—hurdles and tunnels.
- Relay course—multiple handlers and dogs compete together as a team against other teams in a relay race. There are relay pairs (two dogs and two handlers) and relay teams (three or more dogs and handlers). Each dog and handler must perform the course and hand off the baton to the next dog and handler in the team.
- Snooker course—the dog must perform the obstacles (set up in a "standard" or "modified" snooker configuration) according to a particular color pattern. The opening snooker sequence begins where the handler must direct her dog through the obstacles in a "red-color-red-color-red-color" pattern where the "color" is any color object the handler chooses. Each color object has a different point value. Once the dog completes the opening sequence, he finishes with the closing sequence of "yellow-green-brown-blue-pink-black."

Junior handlers will be delighted with their own set of agility titles. USDAA offers Beginning Agility class, Elementary Agility class, Intermediate Agility class, and Senior Agility class.

## Finding a Training Class

You may be feeling overwhelmed after looking at all the agility choices. What organization should you join and what trials should you attend? Before you join any organization, you should perhaps look for a trainer who will help prepare both you and your dog for competition.

By now, you know that there is more to competition than just running obstacles. Agility competition depends on strategy and handling. Finding the right training class will help you on your way

*Michelle training her English Cocker, James, to pause.*

toward competition. Many books, such as my book *Introduction to Dog Agility,* and Jane Simmons-Moake's *Agility Training, the Fun Sport for All Dogs*, cover competition agility training in-depth.

Most agility training classes are offered through obedience trainers or training clubs. Ask your veterinarian, clubs that sponsor agility trials, or other agility handlers where there are good agility instructors. Once you obtain a list, visit those instructors while they are teaching a class. You should visit the training session without your dog to determine if you like and approve of the class and the trainer's style of teaching.

Most trainers hold two types of agility classes. One is the regimented class where everyone works on the same object or handling technique. The other is a drop-in type class where each handler works on what he feels his dog needs. Both types of classes have benefit. The first type of class is regimented and the handlers learn a specific technique or obstacle from the trainer. They get more attention and more focus than they would if they were all training individually. This method is good for beginners and those who need to learn new handling techniques. The downside of this training is that you must work on what the class is working on even if your dog needs practice on another obstacle or technique.

## Checklist for Choosing a Professional Agility Dog Trainer

Does the trainer

- allow you to watch a training session?
- have a regimented class or is it a drop-in type class?
- have enough room for run-throughs or at least sequencing?
- have equipment that's to regulation standard?
- have references?
- own dogs with agility titles?
- compete for titles?
- train you to train your dog?
- use positive methods to train dogs?
- work on obstacles and sequencing?
- have a philosophy that coincides with your own?
- have familiarity with agility?
- teach the style of agility you're interested in?
- treat dogs gently?

The drop-in type class is good for those who need to practice certain techniques they've already learned or to work on a problematic obstacle. While beginners can learn new obstacles in this environment, it may be more difficult than learning in a regimented class setting. The trainer may be assisting someone else while you are trying to teach Sierra the teeter and may need help.

Look for a variety of classes in different facilities. You can learn a multitude of training techniques and gain new insights as to how to train your dog. Not only that, but your dog will become comfortable with diverse equipment and a number of settings—somethings he will need to do if he is at a trial.

## Moving on to Novice

At some point, you'll be thinking about entering your first agility trial. Before you do, if you can, ask someone whose opinion you trust on whether you and your dog are ready for a trial. Trials are stressful both for the handler and the dog and your dog may act up in ways you never thought possible. To avoid embarrassment—and wasting your money—ask someone experienced who has seen you and your dog train. They may give you a brutally honest evaluation, but at least you'll know if you're not ready yet.

Most novice trainers enter their dogs in trials too early. I did, so don't feel like you're alone. When starting out, novice trainers want to show the world how good their dog is. It usually helps to enter a match before plunking down a lot of money to enter a trial.

But how do you enter a trial? You can usually find out about trials through your agility trainer or you can go check online at www.cleanrun.com or www.dogpatch.org. Both of these sites allow you to search for trials and matches in a specific area.

If you've never earned a title on your dog, you'll want to enter the equivalent of the Novice A agility class. Novice A is for those beginning dogs whose handler has never earned a title before. If you're not sure what to enter, contact the trial secretary and ask. He or she can help you fill out your trial form as well.

The good news is that if you try out competition and decide you don't like it, you can still go back to doing agility for fun. After all, that's why you got started in agility in the first place, isn't it?

# Summary

- Many people who start agility for fun get hooked and try competition.
- One type of competition is Just for Fun agility. JFF is a step toward competition and allows you a taste of competing with other agility enthusiasts.
- There are many national and international agility organizations that will allow you to compete with your dog and obtain multiple titles.
- Many agility organizations offer junior, veteran, and difference performance classes.
- Today it is easier for people with disabilities to compete.
- You can earn different titles within an organization, depending on the classes in which you compete.
- When you decide to train for competition, choose a trainer and training facility that match your goals and philosophy in training.
- Before you enter a trial, be sure that your dog is ready.
- If you decide that competition isn't for you, you can always enjoy playing games in dog agility.

# Appendix A
# Agility Organizations

## Amateur Competition

**Just for Fun (JFF)**
8738 Slocum Road
Ostrander, OH 43061
Phone: (740) 666-2018
E-mail: dogwoodbud1@earthlink.net
Web site: http://www.dogwoodagility.com/JustForFun.html

## United States Agility Organizations

**American Kennel Club (AKC)**
5580 Centerview Drive
Raleigh, NC 27606-3390
Phone: (919) 233-9767
E-mail: info@akc.org
Web site: http://www.akc.org

## Australian Shepherd Club of America (ASCA)

P.O. Box 3790
Bryan, TX 77803-9652
Phone: (409) 778-1082
Fax: (979) 778-1898
E-mail: activities@asca.org
Web site: http://www.asca.org

## Canine Performance Events (CPE)

P.O. Box 805
South Lyon, MI 48178
E-mail: cpe@charter.net
Web site: http://www.k9cpe.com

## North American Dog Agility Council (NADAC)

11522 South Highway 3
Cataldo, ID 83810
Phone: (208) 689-3803
E-mail: info@nadac.com
Web site: http://www.nadac.org

## Teacup Dogs Agility Association (TDAA)

P.O. Box 69
Ostrander, OH 43061-0069
Phone: (740) 666-2018
E-mail: dogwoodbud1@earthlink.com
Web site: http://www.dogagility.org

## United Kennel Club (UKC)

100 East Kilgore Road
Kalamazoo, MI 49001-5593
Phone: (269) 343-9020
Fax: (269) 343-7037
E-mail: mmorgan@ukcdogs.com
Web site: http://www.ukcdogs.com

## United States Dog Agility Association (USDAA)

P.O. Box 850995
Richardson, TX 75085-0955
Phone: (972) 231-9700
Fax: (972) 272-4404
E-mail: info@usdaa.com
Web site: http://www.usdaa.com

# International Dog Agility Organizations

This short listing is by no means complete as agility organizations form frequently. If your country isn't listed here, try contacting the Fédération Cynologique Internationale or your national breed club for a list of agility organizations. You may also search the Internet for agility organizations in your area.

## International (General)

### Fédération Cynologique Internationale
Place Albert 1er, 13
B-6530 THUIN
BELGIQUE
Phone : ++32.71.59.12.38
Fax : ++32.71.59.22.29
E-mail : info@fci.be
Web site: http://www.fci.be/home.asp?lang=en

### International Agility Link (IAL)
IAL Global Coordinators
Steve Drinkwater
85 Blackwall Road
Chuwar, Queensland
Australia 4306
Phone: (+61) 7 3202 2361
Fax: (+61) 7 3281 6872
E-mail: yunde@powerup.com.au
Web site: http://www.dogpatch.org/agility/IAL/ial.html

## Australia

### Agility Dog Association of Australia LTD
Cathy Slot, Secretary
85 Blackwall Road
Chuwar, QLD  4306
Phone: (07) 3202 2361
Fax: (07) 3281 6872
E-mail: secretary@adaa.com.au
Web site: http://www.adaa.com.au

## Canada

### Agility Association of Canada (AAC)
RR#2
Lucan, Ontario
N0N 2J0
Phone: (519) 657-7636
E-mail: aac@aac.ca
Web site: http://www.aac.ca

### Canadian Kennel Club (CKC)
89 Skyway Avenue, Suite 100
Etobicoke, Ontario
M9W 6R4
Phone: (416) 675-5511
Fax: (416) 675-6506
E-mail: information@ckc.ca
Web site: http://www.ckc.ca

## Great Britain

### The Kennel Club
1 Clarges Street
London, England
W1J 8AB
Phone: 0870 606 6750
Fax: 020 7518 1058
Web site: http://www.the-kennel-club.org.uk

## Israel

### Agility Club of South Israel
E-mail: agility@inter.net.il
Web site: http://www.geocities.com/Heartland/Park/9576/agility.html

## Luxembourg

### The Agility Club of Luxembourg
Jos Thines, Secretary
43, rue Neuve
3781 Tétange, Luxembourg
Phone: 26 56 07 33
Fax: 26 56 07 34
E-mail: thinesjo@pt.lu
Web site: http://www.agility-ch.ch

# New Zealand

### National Agility Link Association
Karen De Wit, Secretary
74a Kirton Drive
Riverstone Terraces
Upper Hutt, New Zealand
Phone: (04)528-6796
E-mail: kpdewit@xtra.co.nz
Web site: http://homepages.ihug.co.nz/~mbutler/nala/index.htm

# South Africa

### South African Dog Agility Association
Lionel Noik, Managing Director
30 Club Street
Linksfield, Jhb. 2192
Phone: 011 4852100 / 0824564332
Fax: 0114852100
E-mail: lioneln@tiscali.co.za
Web site: http://www.sadaa.co.za

# Appendix B
# Agility References

## Periodicals

**Clean Run**
Clean Run Productions, L.L.C.
35 North Chicopee Street
Chicopee, MA 01020
Phone: (800) 311-6503
E-mail: info@cleanrun.com
Web site http://www.cleanrun.com

**Dog Fancy Magazine**
P.O. Box 53264
Boulder, CO 80322-3264
Phone: (800) 365-4421
Web site: http://www.dogfancy.com

**Dog World Magazine**
P.O. Box 56244
Boulder, CO 80322-6244
Phone: (800) 365-4421
Web site: http://www.dogworldmag.com

# Books and General Reference

Benjamin, Carol Lea. *Second-Hand Dog.* New York: Howell Book House, 1988.

Bonham, Margaret H. *The Complete Guide to Mutts.* Hoboken, N.J.: Howell Book House, 2004.

———— *Introduction to Dog Agility.* Hauppauge, N.Y.: Barron's Educational Series, 2000.

———— *The Simple Guide to Getting Active with Your Dog.* Neptune City, N.J.: TFH, 2002.

Carlson, Delbert G., D.V.M.; and James M. Griffin, M.D. *The Dog Owner's Home Veterinary Handbook.* New York: Howell Book House, 1992.

Coffman, Howard D. *The Dry Dog Food Reference.* Nashua, N.H.: Big Dog Press, 1995.

Coile, D. Caroline. *Beyond Fetch: Fun, Interactive Activities for You and Your Dog.* Hoboken, N.J.: Howell Book House, 2003.

Collins, Donald R., D.V.M. *The Collins Guide to Dog Nutrition.* New York: Howell Book House, 1987.

Daniel, Julie. *Enjoying Dog Agility.* Wilsonville, Ore.: Doral Publishing, 1991.

Eldredge, Deb. *Pills for Pets: The A to Z Guide to Drugs and Medications for Your Animal Companion.* New York: Citadel Press, 2003.

Elliot, Rachel Page. *The New Dogsteps.* New York: Howell Book House, 1983.

Gilbert, Edward M., Jr., and Thelma R. Brown. *K-9 Structure and Terminology.* New York: Howell Book House, 1995.

Hodgson, Sarah. *Dog Tricks for Dummies.* Hoboken, N.J.: Howell Book House, 2000.

Houston, Bud. *The Clean Run Book of Agility Games,* 2nd ed. Chicopee, Mass.: Clean Run Productions, 2003.

Hutchins, Jim. *Do-It-Yourself Agility Equipment: Constructing Agility Equipment for Training or Competition.* Chicopee, Mass.: Clean Run Productions, 2002.

———— *HOGA Agility, Do-It-Yourself Plans for Constructing Dog Agility Articles.* Jackson, Miss.: HOGA Agility, 1999.

James, Ruth B., D.V.M. *The Dog Repair Book*. Mills, Wyo.: Alpine Press, 1990.

Klever, Ulrich. *The Complete Book of Dog Care*. Hauppauge, N.Y.: Barron's Educational Series, 1989.

Mayer, Diane Peters. *Conquering Ring Nerves*. Hoboken, N.J.: Howell Book House, 2004.

Merck and Company. *The Merck Veterinary Manual,* 7th ed. Whitehouse Station, N.J.: Merck and Company, 1991.

O'Neil, Jacqueline. *All About Agility*. New York: Howell Book House, 1999.

Pryor, Karen. *Don't Shoot the Dog! The New Art of Teaching and Training*. New York: Bantam Doubleday Dell, 1999.

Simmons-Moake, Jane, *Agility Training, The Fun Sport for All Dogs*. New York: Howell Book House, 1992.

Smith, Cheryl S., and Stephanie J. Tauton. *The Trick is in the Training*. Hauppauge, N.Y.: Barron's Educational Series, 1998.

Zink, M. Chris, D.V.M., Ph.D. *Peak Performance, Coaching the Canine Athlete*. New York: Howell Book House, 1992.

# Agility Web Sites

The following are agility Web sites that were current as of the writing of this book. Be aware that Internet links appear and disappear frequently.

Agility 4 Fun—http://www.agility4fun.com

Agility Ability—http://www.agilityability.com

Agility Action Online Magazine—http://www.agilityaction.com

Agility Addicts—http://www.agilityaddicts.freeuk.com

Agility in Queensland—http://ourshcltiesite.freeservers.com/agility/agility.html

Agility Net—http://www.agilitynet.com

Agility Workout Society of Mid-Michigan—http://www.awsomm.com

The Agility Zone—http://www.agilityzone.com

American Kennel Club—http://www.akc.org

Barker Dogs—Australian and New Zealand Website—http://barkerdogs.com

Canine Combustion Dog Agility Club—http://www.caninecombustion.com

Canine Sports Productions—http://www.caninesports.com

Dog Dreams (Golden Retriever and Agility Web site)—http://www.dog-dreams.com

The Dogpatch—http://www.dogpatch.org

Dog Play—Having Fun with Your Dog—http://www.dog-play.com

Foxi's Agility Homepage (European Web site with over 8,000 courses)—http://www.agility-ch.ch (click on *Parcours* and then *alle Parcours*)

PawPrint Agility Equipment—http://www.pawprintagility.com

Wellington Hurricanes Flygility Page—http://homepages.ihug.co.nz/~mbutler/hurric.htm

## Agility Equipment on the Web

Affordable Agility—http://www.affordableagility.com

Agility Ability—http://www.agilityability.com

Agility for Less—http://www.agilityforless.com

Champion Tunnels—http://www.championtunnels.com

Dog Equipment.com—http://www.dogequipment.com

eBay—http://www.ebay.com

J and J Dog Supply—http://www.jjdog.com

Max 200—http://www.max200.com

Northwest Agility Products—http://www.nwagility.com

Weave Poles.com—http://www.weave-poles.com

# Picture Credits

# Index

AAFCO (Association of American Feed Control Officials), 133
A-frame obstacle, 46–48, 143
aggressive dogs, non-training, 8
agility organizations, 156–161, 165–169
AKC (American Kennel Club), 6, 9, 157–158
Alaskan Malamute, 74
Algyval liniment, massage, 124–125
allergies, dog food concerns, 137
appetite, health element, 10
Apple Cinnamon Training Bits recipe, 110
ASCA (Australian Shepherd Club of America), 158
attitude, health element, 10
awards, agility party, 114

backchaining, dog walk obstacle, 51
Basset Hounds, agility capable, 7
behavior shaping, clicker training, 30
bicycling, dog/owner activity, 12
bobbing for biscuits, party game, 106
body language, impact on training, 70
body weight, fat examination, 12
Border Collie, handling, 74
bordetella bronchiseptica, 122
breeds, handling differences, 74

canine adenovirus 2, 121
Canine Cookie Bones recipe, 111
canine coronavirus, 122
canine distemper, 121
canine parinfluenza, 122
canine parvovirus, 122
canned foods, pros/cons, 134
cardboard box, special-needs, 144
Carob Treats recipe, 111
chain (chaining), defined, 41
channel method, weave poles, 63
Cheese Nuggets Dog Treats recipe, 110
Chihuahuas, agility capable, 7
chute command, collapsed tunnel obstacle, 56–57
classes/clubs, availability, 7
clicker training
    activity timelines, 27–28
    A-frame obstacle, 46–47
    behavior shaping, 30
    collapsed tunnel obstacle, 56
    command (cue word) addition, 30–31
    dog walk obstacle, 50
    down command, 33–34
    equipment requirements, 24
    fading the lure/target stick, 32
    follow my hands command, 39
    go out command, 36
    go over (hurdles) command, 37–38

clicker training *(continued)*
  go right/left command, 39–41
  here command, 34–35
  hurdle obstacles, 57–58
  introduction techniques, 27–28
  mealtime opportunity, 26
  motivational objects, 35
  noise-making alternatives, 28
  open (pipe) tunnel, 53–54
  operant conditioning, 24, 26
  versus other positive reinforcement
    techniques, 31–32
  pause table obstacle, 60–61
  positive reinforcement, 26
  praise replacement, 26
  response time variation, 28–29
  seesaw (teeter-totter), 52–53
  single dog at a time, 29
  sit command, 33
  target stick introduction, 29–30
  tire obstacle, 60
  treats as praise replacement, 26
  weave pole obstacles, 62–63
clothing, owner/handler guidelines, 17
clubs/classes, availability, 7
collapsed tunnel, 56–57
commands, 30–31, 41
communications, dog/handler obstacle
    directions, 72
competitive agility, 154–156
contact zones, obstacles, 47
courses
  agility party guidelines, 106
  CPE (Canine Performance Events),
    158–159
  eight-obstacle standard, 89, 91
  Flygility, 100
  Gambling Game, 95, 96
  Hound, 95, 98
  jumpers style, 86
  jumpers with weaves style, 86–87
  NADAC (North American Dog
    Agility Council), 159
  puppy agility, 146
  Scavenger Hunt, 98
  Splish-Splash, 95, 97
  standard small area, 89, 90
  Tons o' Tunnels, 92, 93
  tricky sequence with trap, 88

USDAA (United States Dog Agility
    Association), 161
  Weave o' Rama Race, 92, 94
CPE (Canine Performance Events),
    158–159
crawl tunnel, obstacle variation, 63
cross-behind, handling technique, 77
cross-in-front, handling technique, 76
cross-over structure, variation, 63
cue words. *See* commands

disabilities (owner/handler), 7
disabled dogs, special-needs, 147
distracted recalls, party game, 106
dog foods, 131–138
dog walk obstacle, 48–51
down command
  clicker method, 33–34
  in-home training opportunity, 13
  positive reinforcement method, 34
dry foods, pros/cons, 134

ears, health examination element, 9
eight-obstacle standard course, 89, 91
elder dogs, special-needs, 146–147
e-mail, party invitation method, 105
entry point, defined, 70
equipment
  agility party, 109
  clicker training requirements, 24
  course design guidelines, 84–91
  Flygility, 99
  inexpensive alternatives, 7, 19–20
  purchasing versus building, 19–20
  site considerations, 83–84
  special-needs dog modifications,
    143–144
event scheduling, agility party, 113,
    114
exercises, owner's fitness, 17
eyes, health examination element, 9

fading, defined, 32
fetch games, fitness activity, 12
fish crackers, party game, 106
fitness level, pre-training check, 11–12
Flygility
  course elements, 98
  course guidelines, 100

equipment requirements, 99
training techniques, 99–100
flying disc, fitness activity, 12
fly-off, defined, 155
follow my hands command, 39
footwear, owner/handler, 17
four-paw rule, defined, 155
frame command, A-frame obstacle, 47
free feeding, pros/cons, 137
frozen foods, pros/cons, 134, 135
fur, health examination element, 10

Gambling Game course, 95, 96
games, agility party, 106–107
giardiasis, vaccination guidelines, 123
go out command, 35–37
go over (hurdles) command, 37–39
go right/left command, 39–41
Golden Retriever, 74
Great Danes, agility capable breed, 7
greeting cards, party invitation, 105

handling
cross-behind technique, 77
cross-in-front technique, 76
defined, 68
obstacle sequence training, 68–72
on-leash versus off-leash, 67–68
recall over an obstacle, 74–75
right-side versus left-side, 72–74
hand signals, 36
health (dogs)
agility training concerns, 7, 8
examination elements, 9–10
fitness level determinations, 11–12
lameness, 123–129
medication concerns, 127
recurring injury issues, 129
special-needs evaluations, 142–143
vaccinations, 119–123
health (owner/handler), 8
helpers, obstacle training, 52
here command, 13, 34–35
hikes, dog/owner fitness activity, 12
hip dysplasia, 7, 11
holiday/seasonal themes, parties,
102–104
homemade diets, nutritional concerns,
135

hoop tunnel, obstacle variation, 64
Hound course, 95, 98
households, training opportunity, 13
hurdle obstacles, 57–59, 143
hydration, lameness, 124

ice, lameness, 126–127
illness, appetite/attitude indicators, 10
infectious canine hepatitis, 121–122
injury
appetite/attitude indicators, 10
lameness prevention/treatment,
125–129
Internet, party invitation method, 105
invitations, agility parties, 104–105

JFF (Just for Fun) agility, 152–154
judging, agility party criteria, 113–114
jumpers, defined, 84
jumpers style course, 86
jumpers with weaves, 84
jumpers with weaves style course, 86–87
jumps, 37–39

ladders, special-needs dog equipment
modification, 143
lameness, prevention/treatment,
123–129
large breeds, agility capable, 7
left-side handling, obstacle sequencing,
73–74
legs, health examination element, 9
leptospirosis, 122
lifestyles, training requirement adjust-
ment, 7
lyme disease (Borellosis), 123

Malamute, 8, 26
massage, lameness prevention/
treatment, 124–125
match, defined, 153
mealtimes, clicker training opportunity, 26
medications
dog health concerns, 127
lameness treatment, 127
missed contact, defined, 155
mixed breeds, agility acceptance, 6, 9
motivational objects, training aid, 35

mouth, health examination element, 10
musical spots, party game, 107

NADAC (North American Dog
    Agility Council), 159
negative reinforcement, defined, 24
Newfoundland-Samoyed mix, elbow
    dysplasia, 11
nonqualifying run (NQ), defined, 155
nose, health examination element, 10
nose it cue word
    clicker training element, 31
    down command element, 33
NQ (nonqualifying run), defined, 155
nutrition
    dog foods, 131–135
    homemade diets, 135
    performance dog requirements, 136
    table scraps, 138
    treats, 138
    vegetarian diet issues, 138
    water requirements, 134

obstacles
    accident prevention techniques, 56
    A-frame, 46–48
    collapsed tunnel, 55–57
    contact zones, 47
    crawl tunnel, 63
    cross-behind handling technique, 77
    cross-in-front handling technique, 76
    cross-over structure, 63
    dog/handler communications, 72
    dog walk, 48–51
    entry point, 70
    helper positioning, 52
    hoop tunnel, 64
    hurdles, 57–59
    international symbols, 69
    never force your dog, 53
    open (pipe) tunnel, 53–55
    pause box, 64
    pause table, 60–62
    platform jump, 64
    recall over, 74–75
    right-side versus left-side handling,
        72–74
    seesaw (teeter-totter), 51–53
    sequence training, 68–72
    sequencing, 70
    sway bridge, 64

swing plank, 64
tires, 59–60
tower structure, 64
training introduction types, 46
traps, 39, 70
weave poles, 62–63
window jump, 64
wishing well jump, 64
off-course, defined, 155
off-leash handling, dog/owner safety
    issues, 67–68
on-leash handling, dog/owner safety
    issues, 67–68
open (pipe) tunnel, 53–55
operant conditioning
    clicker training element, 24, 26
    defined, 24
over command, hurdle obstacles, 58–59
owner/handlers
    body language impact on training, 70
    clothing guidelines, 17
    exercise considerations, 17
    reasons for agility training, 5–8

parties
    awards, 114
    course planning guidelines, 106
    day-of-activity guidelines, 112–114
    event scheduling, 113, 114
    games, 106–107
    greeting card software, 105
    holiday/seasonal themes, 102–104
    invitation guidelines, 104–105
    judging criteria, 113–114
    planning timelines, 108–109
    prizes, 114
    reasons for hosting, 101
    refreshment suggestions, 108, 114
pause box, obstacle variation, 64
pause table, 60–61
paw it cue word, clicker training
    element, 31
pipe (open) tunnel, 53–55
planks, special-needs dog equipment
    modification, 143
platform jump, obstacle variation, 64
positive reinforcement
    A-frame obstacle, 47–48
    clicker training alternatives, 31–32
    clicker training element, 26
    collapsed tunnel obstacle, 56–57

defined, 24
dog walk obstacle, 50–51
down command, 34
follow my hands command, 39
go out command, 36–37
go over (hurdles) command, 38–39
go right/left command, 42
here command, 35
hurdle obstacles, 58–59
motivational objects, 35
open (pipe) tunnel obstacle, 54–55
pause table obstacle, 61–62
seesaw (teeter-totter) obstacle, 52–53
sit command, 33
tire obstacle, 60
weave pole obstacles, 62–63
praise, clicker training as replacement, 26
prizes, agility party, 114
pumpkin relay, party game, 107
puppies
    agility course guidelines, 146
    agility training timelines, 7, 8, 142–143
    jumping precautions, 37
    Puppy in a Blanket game, 143
    socialization importance, 145
    special-needs training guidelines,
        144–146
    training rules, 144–146
Puppy in a Blanket game, 143

rabies, 120–121
recalls, over obstacles, 74–75
recipes
    Apple Cinnamon Training Bits, 110
    Canine Cookie Bones, 111
    Carob Treats, 111
    Cheese Nuggets Dog Treats, 110
refreshments, agility party, 108, 114
refusal, defined, 155
reproductive organs, health
    examination, 10
response time, clicker training, 28–29
rest, lameness treatment, 127
rest command, contact zones, 47, 48
right-side handling, obstacle
    sequencing, 72–73

Scavenger Hunt course, 98
scramble command, A-frame obstacle, 47
seesaw (teeter) command, 52
seesaw (teeter-totter) obstacle, 52–53

semi-soft foods, pros/cons, 134, 135
sequence, defined, 70
sequencing, defined, 70
shaping, defined, 30, 41
Shetland Sheepdog, 74
sit command, 13, 33
skin, health examination element, 10
small breeds, agility capable, 7
socialization, healthy puppy, 145
sock hop relay, party game, 107
special-needs dogs
    equipment modifications, 143–144
    fitness evaluations, 142–143
Splish-Splash course, 95, 97
standard small area course, 89, 90
stay command, in-home training
    opportunity, 13
straight tunnel, special-needs dog
    equipment modification, 144
stretches, warming up/cooling down
    guidelines, 13–16
sway bridge, obstacle variation, 64
swing plank, obstacle variation, 64
symbols, obstacles, 69

tab, leash alternative, 68
table (pause), 60–62
table command, pause table, 61–62
table scraps, nutrition issues, 138
tail, health examination element, 10
target stick, 29–30, 32
TDAA (Teacup Dogs Agility
    Association), 160
teeter (seesaw) command, 52
teeter-totter (seesaw) obstacle, 52–53
teeth, health examination element, 10
timelines
    agility party planning, 108–109
    clicker training, 27–28
    puppy introduction to agility, 7, 8
tip it command, seesaw (teeter-totter)
    obstacle, 52–53
tippy board, special-needs dog modifi-
    cation, 143
tire command, tire obstacle, 60
tire obstacle, 60
titles, JFF (Just for Fun) agility, 154
Tons o' Tunnels course, 92, 93
touch cue word, clicker training 30
towels, special-needs dog equipment
    uses, 144

tower structure, obstacle variation, 64
trainers, checklist items, 163
training, warming up/cooling down stretches, 13–16
training classes, 161–164
traps, 39, 70
treat hiding, party game, 106
treats
  clicker training element, 26–27
  clicker training fading technique, 32
  nutrition issues, 138–139
  response time variation methods, 28–29
trial
  defined, 153
  novice classes, 163–164
tricky sequence with trap course, 88
T-shirt relay, party game, 107
tunnel command, open (pipe) tunnel obstacle, 53–55
tunnel obstacles, special-needs dog equipment modification, 144

UKC (United Kennel Club), 160
USDAA (United States Dog Agility Association), 160–161

vaccinations
  bordetella bronchiseptica, 122
  canine adenovirus 2, 121
  canine coronavirus, 122
  canine distemper, 121
  canine parinfluenza, 122
  canine parvovirus, 122
  giardiasis, 123
  infectious canine hepatitis, 121–122
  leptospirosis, 122
  lyme disease (Borellosis), 123
  rabies, 120–121
vegetarian diets, nutrition issues, 138
veterinarians
  alternative medicines, 129
  exercise program precheck, 12
  health check elements, 11–12
  vaccinations, 119–123

wait command, contact zones, 47, 48
walk command, dog walk obstacle, 50
walks, dog/owner fitness activity, 12
watch me command, 13
water, nutrition element, 134
Weave o' Rama Race course, 92, 94
weave poles, training, 62–63
Web sites
  agility equipment, 21
  agility trail schedules, 102
  alternative medicine, 129
  clicker equipment, 28
  greeting cards, 105
  JFF (Just for Fun) agility, 152
wide weaves, special-needs dog equipment modification, 144
window jump, obstacle variation, 64
wishing well jump, obstacle variation, 64

Yorkshire Terrier, 74